A JOURNEY OF RICHES

Creating Resilience

A Journey of Riches – Creating Resilience

12 Empowering Stories to Unleash Your Inner Strength

Published by Motion Media International
Editors: Daniel Decillis, Eric Wyman, Yasmin Phillip, Parker Hansen, Rosemary Lawton and Katie Beck.
Cover Design: Motion Media International
Typesetting & Assembly: Motion Media International

Printing: Amazon and Ingram Sparks
Creator: John Spender - Primary Author
Title: *A Journey of Riches – Creating Resilience*
ISBN Digital: 978-1-925919-68-4
ISBN Print: 978-1-925919-69-1
Subjects: Motivation, Inspiration, Memoir

ACKNOWLEDGMENTS

Reading and writing are gifts that very few give to themselves. It is such a powerful way to reflect and gain closure from the past; reading and writing are therapeutic processes. The experience raises one's self-esteem, confidence, and awareness of self.

I learned this when I collated the first book in the *A Journey of Riches* series, which now includes thirty-four books with over 300 co-authors from over 40 countries. Writing about your personal experiences is difficult, and I honor and respect every author who has collaborated in the series.

For many authors, English is their second language, a significant achievement. In creating this anthology of short stories, I have been touched by the generosity, gratitude, and shared energy this experience has given everyone.

The inspiration for *A Journey of Riches, Creating Resilience* was born from my desire to share empowering stories to unleash your inner strength. Each chapter is written by a different author sharing their wisdom on creating the resilience in finding their inner strength.

I want to thank all the authors for entrusting me with their unique memories, encounters, and wisdom. Thank you for sharing and opening the door to your soul so others may learn from your experience. I trust the readers will gain confidence from your successes and wisdom from your failures.

I also want to thank my family. I know you are proud of me, seeing how far I have come from that ten-year-old boy learning to read and write at a basic level. So big shout out to Mom, Robert, Dad, and Merril; my brother Adam and his daughter Krystal; my sister Hollie and her partner Brian; my nephew Charlie and niece, Heidi; thank you for your support. Also, kudos to my grandparents, Gran, and Pop, who are alive and well, and Ma and Pa, who now rest in peace. They accept me just as I am with all my travels and adventures worldwide.

Thanks to the team at Motion Media International; you have done an excellent job editing and collating this book. It was a pleasure working with you on this successful project, and I thank you for your patience in dealing with the changes and adjustments along the way.

Thank you, the reader, for having the courage to look at your life and how you can improve your future in a fast and rapidly changing world.

Again, thank you to my co-authors: Barbara Morris Jensen, Corrina Andersen, Diana Elena Matei, Emily Kane, Sagar Bahadur Dhakal, AJ Myers, Jon Christoffer Henningsen, Kirsten Heynisch, Lars Johansen, Ominda Soemijadi and Inez Cooke.

With gratitude,
John Spender

Praise For *A Journey of Riches* Book Series

"The *A Journey of Riches* book series is a great collection of inspiring short stories that will leave you wanting more!"
~ Alex Hoffmann, Network Marketing Guru.

"If you are looking for an inspiring read to get you through any change, this is it! This book comprises many gripping perspectives from a collection of successful international authors with a tone of wisdom to share."
~ Theera Phetmalaigul, Entrepreneur/Investor.

"*A Journey of Riches* is an empowering series that implements two simple words in overcoming life's struggles.

By diving into the meaning of the words 'problem' and 'challenge,' you will be motivated to believe in the triumph of perseverance. With many different authors from all around the world coming together to share various stories of life's trials, you will find yourself drenched in encouragement to push through even the darkest of battles. The stories are heartfelt personal shares of moving through and transforming challenges into rich life experiences.

The book will move, touch, and inspire your spirit to face and overcome life's adversities. It is a truly inspirational read. Thank you for being the kind, open soul you are, John!"
~ Casey Plouffe, Seven Figure Network Marketer.

"A must-read for anyone facing major changes or challenges in life right now. This book will give you the courage to overcome any struggle with confidence, grace, and ease."
~ Jo-Anne Irwin, Transformational Coach, and Best-Selling Author.

"I have enjoyed the *Journey of Riches* book series. Each person's story is written from the heart, and everyone's journey is different. However, we all have a story to tell, and John Spender does an amazing job of finding authors and combining their stories into uplifting books."
~ Liz Misner Palmer, Foreign Service Officer.

"A timely read as I'm facing a few challenges right now. I like the various insights from the different authors. This book will inspire you to move through any challenge or change you are experiencing."
~ David Ostrand, Business Owner.

"I've known John Spender for a while now, and I was blessed with an opportunity to be in book four in the series. I know that you will enjoy this new journey, like the rest of the books in the series. The collection of stories will assist you with making changes, dealing with challenges, and seeing that transformation is possible for your life."
~ Charlie O'Shea, Entrepreneur.

"*A Journey of Riches* series will draw you in and help you dig deep into your soul. These authors have unbelievable life stories of purpose inside of them. John Spender is dedicated to bringing peace, love, and adventure to the world of his readers! Dive into this series, and you will be transformed!"
~ Jeana Matichak, Author of *Finding Peace*.

"Awesome! Truly inspirational! It is amazing what the human spirit can achieve and overcome! Highly recommended!"
~ Fabrice Beliard, Australian Business Coach and Best-Selling Author.

"*A Journey of Riches* Series is a must-read. It is an empowering collection of inspirational and moving stories full of courage, strength, and heart. Bringing peace and awareness to those lucky enough to read to assist and inspire them on their life journey."
~ Gemma Castiglia, Avalon Healing, Best Selling Author.

"The *A Journey of Riches* book series is an inspirational collection of books that will empower you to take on any challenge or change in life."
~ Kay Newton, Midlife Stress Buster, and Best-Selling Author.

"*A Journey of Riches* book series is an inspiring collection of stories, sharing many different ideas and perspectives on how to overcome challenges, deal with change and make empowering choices in your life. Open the book anywhere and let your mood choose where you need to read. Buy one of the books today; you'll be glad that you did!"
~ Trish Rock, Modern Day Intuitive, Best-Selling Author, Speaker, Psychic & Holistic Coach.

"*A Journey of Riches* is another inspiring read. The authors are from all over the world, and each has a unique perspective to share that will have you thinking differently about your current circumstances in life. An insightful read!"
~ Alexandria Calamel, Success Coach and Best-Selling Author.

"The *A Journey of Riches* book series is a collection of real-life stories, which are truly inspiring and give you the confidence that no matter what you are dealing with in your life, there is a light at the end of the tunnel and a very bright one at that. Totally empowering!"
~ John Abbott, Freedom Entrepreneur.

"An amazing collection of true stories from individuals who have overcome great changes, and who have transformed their lives and used their experience to uplift, inspire and support others."
~ Carol Williams, Author, Speaker & Coach.

"You can empower yourself from the power within this book that can help awaken the sleeping giant within you. John has a purpose in life to bring inspiring people together to share their wisdom for the benefit of all who venture deep into this book series. If you are looking for inspiration to be someone special, this book can be your guide."
~ Bill Bilwani, Renowned Melbourne Restaurateur.

"In the *A Journey of Riches* series, you will catch the impulse to step up, reconsider and settle for only the very best for yourself and those around you. Penned from the heart and with an unflinching drive to make a difference for the good of all, *A Journey of Riches* series is must-read."
~ Steve Coleman, author of *Decisions, Decisions! How to Make the Right One Every Time.*

"Do you want to be on top of your game? *A Journey of Riches* is a must-read with breakthrough insights that will help you do just that!"
~ Christopher Chen, Entrepreneur.

"In *A Journey of Riches*, you will find the insight, resources, and tools you need to transform your life. By reading the author's stories, you, too, can be inspired to achieve your greatest accomplishments and what is truly possible for you. Reading this book activates your true potential for transforming your life way beyond what you think is possible. Read it and learn how you, too, can have a magical life."
~ Elaine Mc Guinness, Best Selling Author of *Unleash Your Authentic Self!*

"If you are looking for an inspiring read, look no further than the *A Journey of Riches* book series. The books are an inspiring collection of short stories that will encourage you to embrace life even more. I highly recommend you read one of the books today!"
~ Kara Dono, Doula, Healer, and Best-Selling Author.

"The *A Journey of Riches* book series is filled with real-life short stories of heartfelt tribulations turned into uplifting self-transformation by the power of the human spirit to overcome adversity. The journeys captured in these books will encourage you to embrace life in a whole new way. I highly recommend reading this inspiring anthology series."
~ Chris Drabenstott, Best Selling Author and Editor.

"There is so much motivational power in the *A Journey of Riches* series!! Each book is a compilation of inspiring, real-life stories by several different authors, which makes the journey feel more

relatable and success more attainable. If you are looking for something to move you forward, you'll find it in one (or all) of these books."
~ Cary MacArthur, Personal Empowerment Coach.

"I've been fortunate to write with John Spender, and now, I call him a friend. *A Journey of Riches* book series features real stories that have inspired me and will inspire you. John has a passion for finding amazing people from all over the world, giving the series a global perspective on relevant subject matters."
~ Mike Campbell, Fat Guy Diary, LLC.

"The *A Journey of Riches* series is the reflection of beautiful souls who have discovered the fire within. Each story takes you inside the truth of what truly matters in life. While reading these stories, my heart space expanded to understand that our most significant contribution in this lifetime is to give and receive love. May you also feel inspired as you read this book."
~ Katie Neubaum, Author of *Transformation Calling*.

"*A Journey of Riches* is an inspiring testament that love and gratitude are the secret ingredients to living a happy and fulfilling life. This series is sure to inspire and bless your life in a big way. Truly an inspirational read that is written and created by real people, sharing real-life stories about the power and courage of the human spirit."
~ Jen Valadez, Emotional Intuitive and Best-Selling Author.

"If you are looking for an inspirational read, look no further than the *A Journey of Riches* book series. The books are an inspiring and educational collection of short stories from the author's soul that will encourage you to embrace life even more. I've even given them to my clients, too, so that their journeys inspire them in life for wealth, health, and everything else in between. I recommend you make it a priority to read one of the books today!"
~ Goro Gupta, Chief Education Officer, Mortgage Terminator, Property Mentor.

Table of Contents

PREFACE

I collated this book and chose authors from around the world to share their experiences about what "Creating Resilience" meant to them. This book is the collective wisdom of the various authors' journeys to unleash their inner strength. This eclectic collection of chapters encompasses many different writing styles and perspectives that embrace the intelligence of our hearts and intuition.

Like all of us, each author has a unique story and insight to share with you. One or more authors might have lived through an experience like one in your life. Their words could be just what you need to read to help you through your challenges and motivate you to continue your chosen path.

Storytelling has been how humankind has communicated ideas and learning throughout our civilization. While we have become more sophisticated with technology and life in the modern world is now more convenient, there is still much discontent and dissatisfaction. Many people have also moved away from reading books and are missing valuable information that can help them move forward with a positive outlook. Moving toward the tasks or dreams that scare us breeds confidence in growing towards becoming better versions of ourselves.

I think it is essential to turn off the television, slow down, read, reflect, and take the time to appreciate everything you have in life. Start with an anthology book as they offer a cornucopia of viewpoints relating to a particular theme. Here, it's fear and how others have dealt with it. We feel stuck in life or have challenges in a particular area because we see the problem through the same lens that created it. With this compendium and all the books in the *A Journey of Riches* series, you have many writing styles and perspectives that will help you think and see your challenges differently, motivating you to elevate your circumstances.

Anthology books are also great because you can start from any chapter and gain valuable insight or a nugget of wisdom without the feeling that you have missed something from the earlier episodes.

I love reading many personal development books because learning and personal growth are vital. If you are not learning and growing, you're staying the same. Everything in the universe is growing, expanding, and changing. If we are not open to different ideas and ways to think and be, then even the most skilled and educated can become close-minded.

This book series aims to open you up to diverse ways of perceiving your reality. It encourages and gives you many avenues of thinking about the same subject. I wish for you to feel empowered to make a decision that will best suit you in moving forward with your life. As Albert Einstein said, **"We cannot solve problems with the same level of thinking that created them."** So, with Einstein's words in mind, let your mood pick a chapter, or read from the beginning to the end and be guided to find the answers you seek.

With gratitude,
John Spender

"Resilience is all about being able to overcome the unexpected."

~ Jamais Cascio

CHAPTER ONE

Sounds of Resilience

Screaming lost to blaring discordant notes;
rushing sound of water tuning out the horror.
Disembodied, my body floats above,
pain no longer felt.
My hand in His, He is my restorer.
Unseen by the abuser, He knelt.
"I will never leave you nor forsake you,
my beloved child."

By AJ Myers

My story begins from childhood and how, unknowingly, a common thread wove through each traumatic event, stitching my life together like a comforting patchwork quilt. I found that thread to be the ingredients of resilience.

Resilience is so much more than simply "pulling yourself up by the bootstraps," although similarly, it is an action. And like many actions, if we listen carefully, there are associated sounds. Once we are intentional about recalling what the associated sounds of trauma are, we can more easily recognize the sounds of resilience and overlay the soundtrack of pain, betrayal, and other traumas. Creating that new sound of resilience helps our mind, body, and spirit to move differently, to dance with abandon and pure joy. This can be freeing.

"'Time heals all wounds isn't necessarily true.
But, there are open paths we can choose to
become resilient and have a life to dream again."
— AJ Myers

* * *

What Right?

What right do I have to discuss resilience?

Surviving experiences that had thrown me down into a deep pit. Traumas beginning from infancy, the loss of my birth parents, hearing for three years that I had no chance to live, transitioning to a new country—a new family—and being persecuted during my childhood. Jarring memories of sexual assault shaking me to my core, being thrust back into my early teenage years pounding down sugary foods and overeating to comfort myself, and not knowing why. Multiple near-death experiences. Losing my best friend—my mother. I was riddled with guilt while at the same time overcome by her loss and bullied into being unable to process my grief. Standing by helplessly as my business burnt to the ground. Being denied a voice and sucking up my feelings because, after all, "AJ is always happy. She has the answer. She's the mediator. Let's go to her because she's a tower of strength."

Not once was I asked how I felt. Nothing but the sound of silence from those who I believed might have cared—who I needed to care.

Deafening, clanging peals sounding the death toll seemed to fill my head. When I learned resilience has specific ingredients, and how to apply them to move past each traumatic event, the soothing sounds of a gentle stream were heard. I spurred on to adjust my mental state to salvage from trouble and learn the importance of surviving and rebuilding the fabric of my life.

What right? My right! I have earned the right to be heard and have this conversation.

* * *

Not Enough

Mom was sitting in her rocking chair while I was exercising, trying to get my adolescent, chubby body to look attractive. I yearned to look like Raquel Welch or Sophia Loren. Amidst my grunting and groaning, Mom stopped rocking. "Dear, no matter how much you exercise, you will never be as beautiful as your sisters. You need to develop beauty within. Develop your mind. In this way, you might become more interesting so boys will look beyond your physical appearance and want to talk with you." As well-meaning as Mom may have been, I struggled for years for my voice to be heard so the absence of beauty would be overlooked. Traumatizing to a young girl. But I didn't scream . . .

Did I scream while being sexually abused as a child or raped as a teenager? No. Nor did I scream during any of the life-threatening incidents I endured thereafter. Fear, humiliation, pain, guilt, and even the sense of inevitability threw me into freeze/retreat mode. Easily startled, that creepy feeling of someone observing me was ever present. Later, I became the victim of stalking. Constantly looking over my shoulder became normalized. Keeping secrets became sacred. Unconsciously, I outwardly became the opposite. Gregarious and talkative, I filled my hours with busyness. I shielded my eyes and ears from all that was ugly. I didn't know why at the time. I just had this near-desperate sense that I had to keep my world safe, beautiful, and filled with joyful sounds. I hadn't yet identified resilience was at play.

Recently, when the heavy protective curtain in my brain pulled apart, exposing deep, hidden traumas in my life, I became hypersensitive to sounds. I was almost blown through the roof. Then, just as quickly, I plummeted into hypo-emotions and feelings. I felt myself shutting down. What I was undergoing is like a balloon quickly losing air or a water bottle being drained of life-sustaining water. All I wanted to do was hide, retreat, and sleep. At that moment, I realized I was experiencing full-blown PTSD and probably had been for some time. Desperate to understand what was happening, I rang the doctor's office for an appointment. She wasn't in. The doctor who did see me immediately ordered a test to be administered, which revealed an alarmingly high depression. Out of genuine concern beyond that of medicine, she suggested I come in on a regular basis just to talk . . . to offload. Because I was able to mask the PTSD for decades, I believed I was able to make resilient choices in the face of trauma. But did I scream? No.

At each point in time, "resilience" did not consciously come to mind. I was broken, tainted/used wares, and therefore felt easily discarded. No matter what I attempted to do to fill in gaping holes or to drown out blaring, ugly sounds attempting to creep in, nothing was ever enough. I lived hidden behind that smiling face, feeling unwanted. I stuffed the worst assaults down deep into the crevasses of my being, mind, heart, and soul. A heavy curtain was drawn closed to deny there was anything to hide that I had been traumatized. The burden was for me to carry; no one to forgive except myself.

However, a sound did break through: a *whisper* that promised I was not alone in this stifling, sad state.

* * *

Trauma & PTSD

"The human capacity for burden is like bamboo
—far more flexible than you'd ever believe at first glance."
— Jodi Picoult, *My Sister's Keeper*

* * *

Many operate with an orphan spirit, feeling unloved and not belonging, searching for nurturing, parental guidance . . . for something more to grasp onto but not knowing what that might be. This leaves us unsure of how to navigate the crumbling rubble caused by pain, betrayal, PSTD, or other trauma to salvage those pieces that will help us to rebuild our lives.

Nina Julia's March 2023 report (https://cfah.org/ptsd-statistics/) on trauma and PTSD provides a look into how Americans are affected:

> ***The leading cause of PTSD is sexual violence at 33%.***
>
> ***3 in 10 or 30% of first responders have PTSD.***
>
> ***11% to 23% of veterans have experienced PTSD within a given year.***

According to her study, 5.6% of traumatized individuals suffer from PTSD worldwide. Booming bells once again clanged loudly within me. I fought the mental urge to slip back into depression. Was there any hope? I sank below the surface of my tub of water in hopes of drowning out the doom of the bells. With these statistics in our face, given these shocking numbers, is there a way to heal from traumatic experiences? The research continued until I found a plausible explanation. Short answer . . .

YES!

RESILIENCE!

Let me begin by saying what resilience is not:

1. Simply holding your head up
2. Pulling yourself up by the bootstraps
3. Slapping a smile on your face

Notable Rockefeller University neuroscientist Bruce S McEwen spent much of his professional career studying and teaching the effects of stress on the brain. His findings further explain how neural circuits and brain structure are reshaped when stress hormones like cortisol are triggered and when neural circuits or BDNF (brain-derived neurotrophic factor) are stimulated with positive input like resilience.

Recently, as of 2020, we are provided a possible explanation for this astonishing finding: "***resilient*** *individuals have reduced interconnectivity among a number of brain regions relative both to controls and maltreated individuals with psychiatric symptoms . . . Teicher interprets this as evidence that secondary changes in specific neural nodes enable* ***resilient*** *individuals to effectively compensate for maltreatment-related brain adaptations."* [emphasis added by author]

"It's not that they are unaffected by maltreatment; rather, their brains are very effectively compensating for it," Teicher says. [The Abused Brain | Dana Foundation]

* * *

Broken Beauty

"Trauma often shatters belief systems and robs people of their sense of meaning. In so doing, it forces people to put the pieces back together *. . . rebuilding beautifully those parts of their lives and life stories that they could never have torn down voluntarily."*
— Jonathan Haidt, *The Happiness Hypothesis*

* * *

Lessons Learned

As the film strip of my life rolls back to its beginning, I see how I have gotten through pain to be where I am today. Peeking into my past, "resilience" wasn't consciously in my purview. I simply did what I needed to survive, unknowingly applying and practicing what I now identify as the ingredients of resilience. Epiphany—light bulb flashing . . . I finally understand my aversions/attractions, the driving force to good and bad choices, and why I am who I am! I should have screamed with revelation, but I remained silent.

Each adverse experience had a common thread running through: Resilience. It wasn't "holding my head up and not allowing my tail to drag between my legs," or "slapping a smile" on my face, as Mom advised. All that did was teach me to ignore and hide my feelings, affix a mask over rose-tinted lenses. Despite how successful I was, something always seemed to raise its ugly head to destroy my relationships. My mother passed away more than thirty years ago, so I no longer can tell Mom, "See? Other people do find me attractive despite you saying throughout my childhood and teenage years, 'too bad you're not as beautiful as your sisters. You'll never catch a man with your looks.'" Resilience got me through every one of those toxic relationships and bad choices and has helped to quiet those hurtful words.

Resilience has lifted me above abusive stepchildren who hated me, whom I took in, raised, cared for, and still love. I have survived an abusive marriage. Hiding from the world, and most importantly from myself, was detrimental to real healing. More than six decades removed from that first assault, I realized that not being able to face some of the gut-wrenching abuses head on has handicapped me from who I was purposed to be. The wonderful thing about resilience is realizing I am free from needing anyone to approve my worth. I am the only one to please with what I've become and who I am.

* * *

Journey of Recovery

Have you experienced an event that was so traumatizing you felt frozen, maybe you were thrown into a time of depression, high anxiety, acquired ulcers, migraines, ill health of some kind, or, like me, became opposite to your true self? You felt/feel you are not enough? There is hope. To really live, and not just survive, I learned to navigate through life's rubble and welcome the sounds accompanying the rebuilding of those broken pieces—the ingredients of resilience must become a part of every fiber of my being.

Part of the sound of resilience is water. I find the sound of water to be healing. Recently, someone I was discussing resilience with likened it to a river. Try as we might to stay in the middle, rough currents push and pull us out of the sweet spot and hurl us towards outcroppings of boulders and other dangers. We fight, squirm, go under and come back up spewing out gobs of water, until finally exhausted, we lie back in total surrender in a relaxed state.

When you let go and allow yourself to go with the flow, the frightening torrent of rushing water becomes the gentle sound of lapping water. You are able to float to that safe place of rest. If you don't, most likely, you will tire mentally, emotionally, physically, and/or spiritually. Maybe have a complete meltdown. When you are tired in one or all these components, you become susceptible to falling prey to illness and disease. Resilience is much like letting go and allowing your mind and body to relax and get back into alignment, floating and going with the flow to stop fighting the rough currents of life.

I spent years trying to prove Mom wrong. Even though I did not scream once while being sexually assaulted or raped, I am no longer in silence. That discordant music has been erased and replaced. "I am free" reverberates throughout my being. I play a new sound . . . a new song reclaiming my resilient destiny.

It's like taking a shower, so you must get to a point where you are willing to wash yourself from those things that are holding you back—words needlessly bouncing around in your head, keeping you from choosing to dress in the ingredients of resilience.

> *"I am so much more than the bad things that are happening to me . . . You can't wait until life isn't hard anymore to decide to be happy."*
> — *Nightbirde* [Jane-AGT 2021]

* * *

What Is Resilience?

Resilience isn't a thing. It is the absence of a thing. This is my take on Dr. David Jeremiah's quote: "Weakness isn't a thing. It's the absence of a thing."

Google "resilience" and a whole plethora of definitions and articles will pop up. "Resilience is the process and outcome of successfully adapting to difficult or challenging life experiences, especially through mental, emotional, and behavioral flexibility and adjustment to external and internal demands" [American Psychological Association]. The key is "*successfully adapting,*" which I find more complex than probably intended.

The *APA Dictionary of Psychology: Building your resilience* states: "Psychologists define resilience as the process of adapting well in the face of adversity, trauma, tragedy, threats, or significant sources of stress—such as family and relationship problems, serious health problems, or workplace and financial stressors . . ."

My mother and father have lived lives absent of succumbing to weakness. They instead allowed resilience to stand in the absence of weakness. They had to be resilient to drown out the cries emanating from the Great Depression, three wars, and thirteen children. My parents were always coming up with ways to keep us engaged, which I now see were lessons in living a resilient life.

One windless summer day, my father called us outside. He began to pull out toys we had never seen from a bag given to him by an Australian sailor. Among them were boomerangs. I stood there amazed as he tossed the boomerang away from him, only for it to turn around and come back without falling to the ground. In similar fashion, we often react to extreme situations like the boomerang: stopping during our forward motion in life, only to abruptly return to that trauma.

Do you think a gecko or any lizard whose tail grows back after it is ripped off from being caught in the clutches of a hunter is resilient? What about the dreaded cockroach? When my husband took the children and me to the Midwest to meet his family, our first stop was dinner at a Sonic Drive-in. Night descended while we sat at the table. Fluorescent tubes flickered on. Suddenly, our air space was inundated with flying insects, muffling our conversation with their humming. Big, creepy things that you do not want to accompany your meal were dive-bombing. A giant flying cockroach landed right next to us. My husband's middle son stomped on the bug with his size 10 shoe. We all squealed at the loud, gross crunching sound. When he lifted his foot, this squashed cockroach puffed itself back up and took off with its wings intact. Was that resilience?

Elasticity. How many of us have taken a rubber band and stretched it as far as we could then let go? Is that moment of decision when we rise again and snap into our physiology and mental well-being, our emotions and our spirit propelling us forward, resilience? I do believe resilience is somewhat like the rubber band stretched and stretched until we let go.

Okay, so let's look at each of the ingredients of resilience.

* * *

Ingredients of Resilience

The ingredients of resilience I learned are:

1. Acknowledgement: Face the circumstance, no matter if fear or shame is felt. Call it out for what it was/is. Acknowledge you do not have to be alone and may need help from trusted allies.
2. Forgiveness: Be willing to forgive yourself and your feelings, your thoughts. Forgive whoever caused you grief—not necessarily for them, but for you so you can have peace.
3. Faith: Know that by claiming an unwavering faith, you will live. You will heal. You have the strength to restart or create new dreams.
4. Grace: Give yourself grace to move through trauma. Grace is addictive and can spill over to others.
5. Hope: During your journey to move past explosive situations, keep hope in front of you. Hope helps to sustain you when your journey gets bumpy. Hope keeps your dreams real.
6. Love: There is no better revenge than to love. We are called to love our enemies. A change will begin in the pit of your gut when you practice and extend love towards others and yourself. Bitterness will be uprooted and die. Love thaws a frozen heart or mind. Love will set in motion a healing energy that touches your brain's neurology (specifically, the "brain-derived neurotropic factor" [BDNF]) and help heal your cell membrane. You will learn to love others and accept love in return, that there is no false version of love.

When you are willing to apply and practice all these ingredients no matter what you have gone through, are going through, or may go through, you will find a source of strength to be fully resilient.

Embracing the ingredients of resilience may look different for each of us because our stories are uniquely our own. I find it helpful to ask, "What do I think puts me into a place of having to be resilient?" Then I mark how I applied the ingredients of resilience. What did it take? What was the cost for me? You might want to ask yourself the same.

Whether you know consciously or unconsciously, imbued within you is resilience. The beginning of claiming a resilient life is acknowledging you can't always go it alone. For me, knowing I can stand on the shoulders of my Lord and Savior to carry the weight allows me to live resiliently.

* * *

Characteristics of Resilience

Resilient people share the ability to employ strong coping skills. They look to helpful resources and aren't afraid to ask for needed assistance to ultimately find ways to make sense of their feelings and prioritize how to manage the crisis situations they are in. Although how they practice coping skills may look different, the fact that they intentionally choose to use these empowering skills creates strong functionality in mind, body, and spirit.

James Woodsworth's article "Are You Surviving or Thriving?" (posted on psychreg.org) noted that "Resilience is often referred to as the ability to bounce back from adversity." He further states, "Thriving following a traumatic event, as already mentioned [sic] is not necessarily easy, in fact in many respects it can be incredibly challenging but it is nevertheless possible – it's just a question of the attitude we choose to take towards the situations we face."

James Woodworth shares in a separate article, "What Are the Characteristics of Resilient People and How to Develop Them," published 28 October 2016 on psychreg.org:

1. *Develop an internal focus of control*
2. *Develop high self-esteem*
3. *Develop high self-efficacy*
4. *Develop good self-awareness and good emotional management*
5. *Develop optimism and hope*
6. *Develop positivity and positive emotions*
7. *Develop gratitude and appreciation*
8. *Develop a SMART attitude to goal-setting*
9. *Develop a flexible and adaptable attitude*
10. *Develop a positive, optimistic explanatory style*

Kendra Cherry, whose expertise lies in psychology, child psychology, personality, and research states, *Resilient people take responsibility for their thoughts, feeling and actions. However, they are unlikely to blame themselves unnecessarily nor do they see bad things as infiltrating every aspect of their lives. They have perspective.* [Kendra Cherry, MSED posted on very well mind | Oct 06, 2022]

Read that again: "unlikely to blame themselves . . ."

Often, when encountering a resilient person, the general belief is that person is free of the distress, grief, anxiety, or depression that others who share a similar trauma have. This is not so. What is true is that resilient people do not hide, refusing to face fear or crisis. Similar to my parents, they instead used empowering and healthy coping skills to foster an inner strength, learning and growing from the experience. Here are some strategies that I find help develop or increase resilience:

- Create healthy connections with empathetic people whom you can trust and unload your feelings to without the fear of judgement.

- Become active with a faith-based group, other supportive groups, or a volunteer group so the focus is off you and on helping others.
- Foster a wellness plan to take care of your mind, body, and spirit. Remember to recall and focus on those things you are grateful for. Visit your wellness plan frequently and tweak it as necessary. (I create a daily thankful or grateful list. This has been particularly important during times of great loss, illness, and challenges.)
- Recognize triggers that may include unhealthy choices to mask unpleasant feelings. Stay away from temporary band-aids. Refocus on your wellness plan to propel you towards healthy goals you determined for yourself.
- Keep perspective when identifying irrational thinking and adopt a more balanced thinking pattern that aligns with reality. You are not helpless. You can change how you react/respond to your interpretation.
- Flame hope even when life may be misdirecting you. A memorized verse, phrase, mantra, or word is important. Say it out loud so you hear your voice reaffirming hope. This will cause positive neuro-sensory vibrations.
- Remember to check in with yourself. How are you feeling? What are you feeling?
- Remind yourself that you are powerful.
- Visit your past and pull out what was helpful for you to get through something you thought was impossibly difficult. Even in the direst of circumstances, something positive can be gained and applied to a current or future event to help you.

Proverbs 3:5–6 is a good passage to cling to whenever I am experiencing a challenge or can see only disaster ahead:

"*Trust in the Lord* with all your heart,
and lean not to your own understanding.
In all your ways acknowledge him,
and he shall direct your paths."

I dearly hope you will accept that how you see yourself and the choices you make to accept who you are will define how you live your life and how you treat others and will set your feet on a path of limitless, resilient possibilities.

* * *

Choosing Resilience

I am pretty sure, like me, you have often heard the word "choice." There is nothing truer than when I tell you: resilience, like a muscle, relies on making an intentional, functional choice, then consistently practicing that choice. The question is, will you choose to embrace and intentionally practice resilience, so it becomes a part of you for life? I encourage you to apply it to the past, the present, and/or the future you are *trying* to get through. Be intentional.

Taking this information and making resilience a habit will determine the steps you take forward in life. Believe resilience will get you through the storms of life. Breathe in deeply this belief. When you fully embrace resilience, you activate neurological strands of energy that can touch others who may also need uplifting. This positive, resilient state affects the type of people who will be attracted to you so you can be elevated—not pulled down. Based on the Rockefeller studies, I ask myself, is this how I have managed to cope and show the world a smiling, successful person in the face of horrific experiences?

Was I a victim? Yes.

Am I a survivor? Yes.

However, I choose not to live in survival mode, but as a free, empowered, and resilient person. I survived by embracing all the ingredients of resilience not only to get through, but to help others walk the path to wholeness—begin building bridges to be resilient and move beyond the pain, the loss, the guilt, the sorrow—begin to claim a new life. I do believe Jesus's constant presence and God's hand upon me allowed my brain's specific neural nodes to compensate for maltreatment-related brain adaptations in every traumatic event I suffered through. This is how the ingredients of resilience were then scribed upon my mind and heart.

Circling back to the muscle analogy, increasing resilience takes time and intentionality. In other words, you must work at being resilient and choose to make resilience your normal. Once resilience becomes your norm, you will find that it is the heartbeat of leadership, of getting through tough times so you can soar. You can be free from that which has anchored you down. I challenge you to silence the screams of terror and exchange them for the sounds of joy. A new choice will present itself . . . a new journey.

Here is an exercise to help get unstuck from your debilitating narrative:

Part I

- Be in a safe space.
- Get comfortable.
- Allow your breathing to slow.
- Close your eyes.
- Think of the worst scenario that happened to you.
- Use all your senses of sight, sound, touch/feeling, and smell to get into that moment. Taste the bitter poison of imprisonment.

- Notice the lighting, the weather, sounds, and how you are feeling.
- Completely be immersed in this event.
- Keep your eyes closed.
- Now touch your left knee.

Part II

- Keep your eyes closed.
- Notice how you are feeling and breathing.
- Relax your body.
- Relax your shoulders.
- Ensure your feet are uncrossed, making sure to place them flat on the ground if you are sitting.
- Shake out any tension in your arms and your hands.
- Allow yourself to go back to a time when you, without a doubt, were resilient.
- Notice again all your senses—where were you? Put color and shape to your feelings. Taste the sweetness of release from the incapacitating clutches of imprisonment.
- Breathe in your empowerment.
- Notice your mindset and what you did to get unstuck and move forward.
- With your eyes still closed, touch your right knee.

By completing Part II, you overlay the negative with the positive. You re-fuse that part of your brain stuck in pain with resilient power. Research has found there are several ways in which to release the natural substance known as "brain-derived neurotropic factor" (BDNF) which triggers the brain's ability to transmit signals from neuron to neuron by way of growing new synaptic connections. Negative vs positive. These could be experiences, actions/movement, words, and/or feelings. Nerve cells are weakened and even strangled by trauma, stress, and deprivation, whereas intentional movement—taking action, forgiveness, and love—strengthens BDNF. In other words, when you choose to give yourself permission to have a new narrative, you trigger BDNF to stimulate growth—to fuse new neuropathways to create a new, resilient you.

After you have completed this exercise, claim a song that will help you reset if you find the discordant noise creeping back in. Your song can also keep you moving along your resilient journey. I have two songs: "Say I Won't" by MercyMe, and "We Will Rise" by NDLOVU Youth Choir from Limpopo S Africa (this song is about the reliance of the human spirit).

* * *

A Worthwhile Exercise

The following worksheet is provided by Psychology Today (www.psychologytoday.com):

Worksheet: "It Could Be Worse . . ." is an exercise to help you apply this approach.

Complete this exercise by answering each question at your own pace. As you work through the activity, try to imagine yourself in the situation you're writing about, as vividly as you can.

Step One:

Describe a situation that you're currently struggling with.

1. *What is most challenging about this situation, in your opinion? What aspects of this situation are hardest for you to deal with right now?*

2. *Can you identify any particular thoughts that are bothering you? e.g., "If only . . ."*

Step Two:

Now, try to shift your focus away from the specifics of the situation. Instead, try to brainstorm three ways the situation could be worse.

Write out your responses, trying your best to fully imagine yourself in that scenario as you write.

1. *How could it be worse? Identify three ways this situation could be more difficult.*

For the full article and other worksheets, visit: www.psychologytoday.com.

* * *

For You

"The oak fought the wind and was broken, the willow bent when it must and survived."
— Robert Jordan, *The Fires of Heaven*

Life isn't fair. Justice isn't always served as hoped. You can't always control what happens. You may not be able to change the past, but you can control how the associated feelings, sights, and sounds can be altered. Be empowered and practice resilience until you form this positive habit like you would if you were exercising your muscles. You will find that no matter what happens, you can choose to pick up the thread of resilience that weaves through each circumstance and stitch your unique fabric of life into one gloriously patterned quilt.

Listen to your unique sounds of resilience. You can find your voice and speak up. You deserve to be heard. Do so from the position of empowerment and not from a victim's scream. Reclaim who you were meant to be—who you are. Re-dream BIG. Be unstoppable. Consistently and intentionally strive upward and onward, so your dreams can become your resilient reality. Weave into your legacy the joyful sounds you hear when the ingredients of resilience are fully ingrained into your life.

* * *

Fabric of Life

What color do you see?
What color do I see?
Are they different? Can they be the same?
Does this really matter?
I say, embrace all the colors and fabrics of your life.
You get to design your resilient outcome.

"No one escapes pain, fear, and suffering. Yet from pain can come wisdom, from fear can come courage, from suffering can come strength – if we have the virtue of resilience."

~ Eric Greiten

CHAPTER TWO

An Ocean of Innate Resilience

By Lars Johansen

INTRODUCTION

One of the classic metaphors for resilience in life involves ocean waves. Our psychological and emotional experiences can be viewed as waves that wash through us; we are the ocean containing all these waves. However, we are neither defined nor restricted by them. If we can simply remember that we are the ocean, there is no need to fear the waves. But when we forget we are the ocean, we may suffer. And we certainly know how easy it is to forget. How easy it is to forget our true nature. All it takes is one negative experience.

Research indicates that we are exposed to significant stress factors an average of three to four days a week. These may range from the head teacher phoning you to talk about your son's behavior to you forgetting your cell phone when leaving work, or discovering that someone dented your car in the car park without leaving their name and phone number.

Everyone wants emotional resilience to enable them to safely navigate challenging and stressful events and overcome setbacks as quickly as possible. To quote Rick Hanson, "The brain is like Velcro for negative experiences and Teflon for positive ones." We are hardwired by evolution to focus on negative experiences. For something positive to be committed to long-term memory, we must be cognizant of and present in these experiences for at least fifteen to thirty seconds. As this rarely occurs, most positive experiences flow through the brain like water through a sieve, while negative ones are often captured and stored.

The good news, however, is that you have internal tools and strategies you can use at any time to redirect your thoughts from feelings of stress towards more appropriate ways of coping with stress factors in your life. This will help improve your inner strength and make you happier and more emotionally resilient. The more emotionally resilient you become, the more often you experience positive emotions, the better you become at remaining emotionally stable through adversity, and the faster you re-establish positive emotions after setbacks. Not only that, but emotional resilience can help you gain access to more creativity, intelligence, wisdom, and love.

Resilience is a natural part of life. It is a neuroplastic process that strengthens you when you're not doing well. It is the ability to improve your relationship with stress. You have seen it in action in others and have experienced it in yourself. It is neither something you do, nor something you accomplish. It happens all by itself when you're free from unnecessarily restrictive thinking, a little like using a clutch to shift gears on a car. You must first disengage the old gear to change into a new gear. Or, as Albert Einstein said, "We can't solve problems by using the same thinking we used when we created them."

In this chapter, you will meet fifteen-year-old Leah, who was shocked when she contacted the Emergency Room for help with a red rash on her back. It turned out to be something completely different, and this is her story of tapping into her natural innate resilience.

Roros, Norway, 7th of October 2022

The phone rings, and I answer. On the other end is Leah, my daughter.

"Hi, Leah! How are you doing?" I hear heavy breathing in the background, which first makes me think this is a pocket dial, but it isn't.

And then I hear: "DAD … DAD … (heavy crying on the other end) I've been to the emergency room. The doctor says I have diabetes. Type 1 diabetes. He's taken many tests and discussed the case with colleagues at St. Olav's Hospital in Trondheim. They're sure I have diabetes. The test shows I have abnormally high blood sugar. They say I need to come right away since ketoacidosis is dangerous. Mom and I are packing a bag and taking a taxi to Trondheim in a couple of minutes. Can you come too?" she asks.

"Of course, I can, Leah! I may not make it until tomorrow morning, but I'm coming," I tell her as a thousand questions run through my head. I know they'll have to wait until later.

"Dad! Is there something wrong with me? I'll never be myself again, will I?" she half-asks, half-concludes.

I take in the despair, the confusion, and, not least, the shock of her life being turned completely upside down. The last thing I do before hanging up is assure her there's nothing wrong with her. She had no idea how much resilience she would gain from this major setback in her life.

At St. Olav's Hospital the following day, we meet a cheerful, relaxed, knowledgeable pediatrician specializing in diabetes. He tells us that Leah has developed type 1 diabetes—an incurable condition she will have to live with for the rest of her life.

It struck me that very few parents prepare their children for life's unpredictable and inevitable setbacks. It's a conversation that usually occurs after something difficult or disappointing happens. We are much better in our society at making contingency plans for disasters and pandemics but significantly worse at preparing our children for life's disappointments, setbacks, and hardships. That includes articulating that the benefit of these challenges is a greater sense of resilience, tolerance for adversity, and one's ability to see the gift in every situation.

Leah was trapped in her lower brain. She was overwhelmed and frightened by meter-high waves of fear, and she fought desperately against the swell of sadness, grief, and anger. It was painful to see her suffer like this, but at the same time, I knew it was a subtle balance between succumbing to the temptation to make decisions for her and letting her take the stairs up to her higher brain on her own. I was never worried that she wouldn't recover from the disappointment and shock because it's our nature to recover, just like when the corn lays on the farmer's field after the autumn storm. It can look as if the corn has broken, but as soon as the sun rises, it can grow and stretch up towards the life-giving sun. That is the natural and innate resilience of corn.

After the meeting with the pediatrician, I wanted to create a space where it was safe for her to be calm, where she could feel confident that the love and connection to me as a parent existed no matter what happened on the outside.

"On a scale of one to ten, where ten is very good and one is very bad, how are you feeling right now, Leah?"

She looks up at me with tears and replies, "Very bad, Dad."

"I know. Shall we do something that makes you happy?" I say with a slightly more optimistic tone.

"Can't we just walk along the river," she says.

"Of course we can," I say, giving her a hug and a kiss on the forehead. Hand in hand, we walk along the edge of the river and breathe in the cold autumn air. We're both paralyzed by the beautiful orange, yellow, and red uniformed oak trees preparing for a shift to a colder season.

After a while, she says, "Let's sit on the bench by the riverside. I need to rest."

"Sure. Let's do it," I say and sit down next to her. Almost like in meditation, we sit quietly, just breathing and enjoying the silence, listening to the wind create a calming, repetitive sound when it hits the colorful leaves in the trees around us. "I've never told you that the human design is perfect with an amazing ability to bounce back after we have experienced defeat, setbacks, or adversity," I say to her. "It's our reservoir of innate resilience."

I explain to Leah, "what's been helpful for me, and many of my clients through challenges and life crises, has been a mindful exercise called "Hand on the heart." It's maybe the fastest way to down-regulate the stress response and reduce the flow of cortisol in your body. Warm touch activates the release of oxytocin, the hormone of safety and trust. Oxytocin is the brain's direct and immediate antidote to the stress hormone cortisol; it returns our brain to a state of equilibrium and brings the functioning of the higher brain back online. It's straightforward. Everyone can do it. It's the perfect tool to enhance your innate resilience to cope with mini meltdowns.

Find a quiet place where you won't be interrupted. You can even place some pillows behind your back and sit comfortably in your bed with your eyes closed if you want to. Focus for a few moments on your breathing to get into a relaxed state of mind.

Place your hand over your heart and notice how the area begins to feel warmer. Now imagine how that warmth slowly grows, covering your chest and belly.

Now you can say some reassuring phrases to yourself: "May I be well. May I be safe. May I be happy. May I be healthy. May I find peace today." Bask in the feeling of loving kindness for a few minutes. And if your mind starts to wander, bring your attention back to the warm feeling from the oxytocin floating through your body.

If you want to, you can extend your compassion to someone you care about. Imagine a good friend, grandma, mom, dad, a boyfriend, or your beautiful cat, and let your love for them grow. Send your loved one positive thoughts by repeating the exact calming words you gave yourself:

"May you be well. May you be safe. May you be happy. May you be healthy. May you be at peace today." If you do this exercise several times a day, your brain will get used to going there because our brains learn 'little and often'; the brain learns best from small experiences repeated many times. First, you do it for a week and continue until it develops into a healthy habit," I say, and notice Leah has placed her hand over her heart.

Interestingly, research shows that being held by someone we feel safe with, even being physically near someone we feel safe with, even imagining being with someone we feel safe with, is enough to release the oxytocin that will restore our physiological equilibrium, bringing us back into a state of calm and trust from which it is possible to be resilient.

My family's next few days are devoted to learning about the nature of the disease and how to use necessary medical devices such as an insulin pen and insulin pump. Leah also learns how to calculate the quantity of carbohydrates in the food she eats and the correct insulin dose for each meal. We are also given access to an app for tracking blood sugar levels throughout the day, which the entire family can use.

The next day after lunch, we walk along the river, past the famous Nidaros cathedral, over the bridge called "The Portal of Happiness," and back to the hospital, a round trip that takes an hour and a half. We usually stop at the same bench for a chat. "I can feel something is bothering you. Is it something you want to share with me?" I ask her.

She's got a sad look in her eyes. "I'm so scared that my friends and everyone else will start looking at me differently—like there's something wrong with me. Someone with a disability, someone they want nothing to do with. I'm terrified the disease will ruin me," she says, turning to see my reaction. I am impressed with how well she is able to express her feelings, a sign that her flow of innate resilience is ready for activation.

"I know it can be difficult, so early in the course of the disease, to look at type 1 diabetes through positive glasses, and I wouldn't have suggested it if I didn't know that you are a reflective and sensible girl. Should we see what happens when we turn negative into positive?"

She snorts (in frustration) and shrugs in response. Leah struggles initially to see something positive in the disease, but her perspective gradually improves. Another tell-tale sign that someone isn't blocking their innate resilience is their ability to transform a negative into a positive, calibrating the experience. Here is some of what she came up with in her initial round of doing the exercise:

'Of the more than ten thousand diseases I could get, type 1 diabetes is one of the better ones I could get. Many have it far worse than me.'

'I am lucky to have a professional diabetes team that accompanies me and from whom I can ask for advice if I want.'

'The pediatrician says that the disease is incurable, but some people have changed their diet to vegan and cured themselves. There are also several trials for treatments to reverse type 1 diabetes and restore the body's ability to produce insulin naturally. I hope there will be a cure within a few years.'

'I can live well with a disease like type 1 diabetes. The pediatrician says I can do everything I've done before, including eating a piece of cake, even chocolate and ice cream. I have to be careful to put in the correct insulin dose when I eat and consider doing physical activity. I let go of all negative emotions and move on in life.'

'If my friends accept me even though I have type 1 diabetes, they like me for who I am.'

Eight months later, in June 2023, here's what she shared with me, demonstrating her enhanced, free-flowing innate resilience:

'After I got diabetes, I have become much more grateful for small things. Things that previously seemed small and insignificant are now big and important to me. Previously, taking a shower could be something I squeezed into a hectic schedule. Today, I enjoy and appreciate the warm drops of water that hit my skin, perfectly soft and warm. I can think about the cycle of water that right now gives me a wonderful moment of well-being before it disappears down the drain and embarks on a new circuit.'

'After I got the disease, I have also become gentler with myself and others. I rather look for what is going well than what is going wrong. I also try, to a greater extent, to bring kindness to situations that are difficult or painful. I know that over time, that painful experience can enhance our ability to recognize our innate resilience.'

'I am not alone in the world in having an inner critic who feeds me with negative self-talk, but like the background noise in a café, it's up to me whether I want to be annoyed by it. I choose to ignore everything that is not love.'

Before Leah reached the free-flowing stage of her innate resilience, there were quite a few mini meltdowns. Leah was in regular contact with her best friends; they had agreed to meet her at the hospital during the week, but a message on Snapchat changed everything.

"Do you know what my friends are doing?! They're not coming to see me at the hospital! I can't believe it! They're taking the train to Oslo! Are you listening? And do you know what they're going to do there? They're going to a café, to a restaurant, shopping, and staying with some people they know," she says, counting these things on her fingers, "while I have to spend my holiday at the hospital! Hello?! You do realize it's autumn break. Autumn break, Dad! I don't have time for this! Can't we check with the pediatrician to see if we can finish tomorrow? I want to go home!"

It's amazing what an embrace and body heat does to the nervous system. When I struggled with panic attacks some years ago, placing a hand over my heart could calm the panic attack in less than sixty seconds. It was incredibly effective. Now, embracing Leah has the same effect. It down-regulates her nervous system, calms her down, and integrates her higher brain, bringing her back to the safety zone. I wipe a few tears from her cheek and explain that teenage brains don't have a fully developed higher brain yet. I tell her that sometimes teenagers act before they think, which is probably the explanation for why her friends chose to go to Oslo instead of visiting her. In retrospect, they will see that they should have visited Leah instead. Kindness is one of the significant demonstrations of higher brain development and free-flowing innate resilience.

The days fly by. Between physiotherapy and appointments, it is liberating and relaxing to spend quality time with my daughter, sitting on the bench by the river's edge.

I explain to her that the intention of the survival part of your brain isn't to ruin things for you; it just wants to protect you, take care of you, and make sure you feel okay. "That's why it scans your surroundings, so it can get any situation under control as quickly as possible—without paying attention to anything else. But it will never be able to help you accept a situation as it is. Therefore, the solution lies in the interval between thoughts and reactions. This is where you can change your thinking, allowing something new to come in.

"If you're experiencing something complex and frightening, take a break. Breathe, pay attention, and tell yourself: 'I see you, anger. I see you, fear. I see you, grief. I'll be here with you until you go away.' If you observe the emotion and leave it alone rather than identify with it, you are reacting in the moment and can avoid suffering. When you see a wave, it becomes the ocean. You can respond calmly to the wave because you're not trapped inside it. Through regular practice, you develop the resilience to respond rather than react. That's the doorway to freedom.

"Acceptance only happens when you are present, in the here and now. This is hard for many people to accept. It's not easy. I'll be the first to admit that it was challenging to acknowledge that Mom had found a new man to be with. It was painful knowing she wanted to be with someone other than me. It was also horrible to see that you, Mom, your little brother, and I would no longer live under the same roof. That part of my life was over. It was painful to know that I would no longer experience all those big and small moments with all of you. No more birthdays. No more holidays. No more Christmas Eve. It was over—the end.

"There were many sleepless nights and a lot of tears. It was a massive test of my ability to tap into my innate resilience. Things like that affect us deeply, all these sensitive threads burrowing deep into our subconscious. And when someone pushes the right buttons, it retrieves memory and triggers an emotional reaction. For me, it was the grief of losing my family. To bounce back after the breakup, I paid more attention to the positive experiences we have had together than the sadness, anger, and anxiety I also felt. Gratitude, hope, and love gave me the strength to come out of the grief and to be able to start anew with blank pages. Knowing you are resilient is when you can accept the situation and focus on what you can control, which is how you respond.

"For instance, you were annoyed and frustrated just now about having been diagnosed with type 1 diabetes, and you were really angry about having to be at the hospital while your friends were enjoying themselves in Oslo. When you identify with the situation, you leave the moment—you lose yourself and pay the price in the form of suffering.

"Acceptance requires you to put in some effort. It requires you to open your eyes. To wake up. To be curious. To be 'here,' mentally present in the timeless NOW. Not 'there'—when it happened—or at a moment that hasn't happened yet. Only in the HERE and NOW can you accept and move on. This doesn't mean that you should accept something awful that someone says or does; it just means that you accept things as they are. NOW is all we have. We can leave out what comes after and accept the NOW—it's where your superpower, your resilience, is fortified, and you can be solution focused.

"What I'm trying to say is: I want you to accept the condition for now. Because then you can use the energy you would otherwise have wasted on being angry about the disease, so you can do your best to have a fantastic life and use your resourcefulness to get an education, have a career, move into your own home, take care of your friends and family, and perhaps eventually find someone special to settle down with.

"As for the first thing you said—your fear that you're not good enough, that your friends will turn their backs on you and not want anything to do with you—relax, don't worry. That won't happen. You are incredibly kind, considerate, generous, loyal, helpful, and funny. There's always something fun happening in your life, and you're also an extremely good friend, Leah.

"But remember, putting your oxygen mask on first before helping others is always a good idea. You need to take care of yourself, first and foremost. Don't ignore yourself, thinking that being your own best friend is selfish, because that's not true. People who are kind to themselves, who treat themselves with understanding and compassion, will grow, flourish, feel more motivated and recover faster after experiencing setbacks. Remember, you are the ocean; you're not an anxious wave. Come back to your true nature; your wave is resilience itself."

I get to my feet. "Now let's take some of that delicious bread we got from the hospital, bread that would otherwise have been thrown out, and give it to our friends down by the river—to the ducks, the seagulls, the crows, and the other birds. You know how good it feels to be caring and giving?" I ask.

Leah nods and smiles.

As we begin to feed the birds I continue our talk "Well, that's the wonderful thing about compassion. Suppose we practice it often enough and care about other people, animals and birds, nature, the environment, and the earth. In that case, it will all come naturally, and we will become the kind of person who gives without expecting anything in return. Compassion also reduces distress, depression, and feelings of loneliness, increases positive emotions, and promotes emotional well-being, all enhancing compassion resilience. But you know what, I've talked enough for now. You and I deserve to have a coffee—don't you agree? Because my bag is empty."

I shake out the last remaining breadcrumbs while a couple of pigeons launch themselves at them.

"YES! That's the best thing you've said all day! Thanks, Dad!" says Leah, and she almost dies laughing.

This heartfelt, liberating laughter is contagious. Leah orders iced coffee, toast, and a piece of cake, quickly calculating how much insulin she needs to inject. She has adapted to this new routine and habit in record time and doesn't appear to be significantly inhibited by the disease. I am very impressed and proud of the way she has picked up new knowledge and adapted to a new daily routine with a smile on her face.

I feel immensely grateful for and humbled by these seven unexpected days—which I would have never had the chance to experience had she not become ill. Every day has been a gift. We don't usually consider an incurable disease a gift. It makes me think of when Jesus met the Pharisee Nicodemus. To see the kingdom of God, he had to be born again. To see the big picture, you must be willing to let go of your personal, psychological, plaintive, judgmental, and limiting self. When you learn to see not only with your eyes but also with your heart, then whatever you have perceived as ugly, destructive, harmful, or hopeless can become something else entirely in an endless sea of opportunities. From the perspective of your true nature, the ocean sees and includes all waves, our source of innate resilience.

If you are looking for gifts, it is gifts you will find. It took 27 years for Nelson Mandela to be released from prison, but instead of being obsessed with thoughts of revenge and violence, he was full of forgiveness and compassion. Nelson Mandela knew that love always wins over hatred and violence. Now that's resilience!

Several research studies and advances in neuroscience indicate that practicing gratitude provides a broad range of benefits for our emotional and physical well-being. A gratitude practice, for instance, writing a gratitude journal, will give you more energy, make you more optimistic, improve your mood, boost your sense of well-being, build more resilience, raise your self-esteem, improve your relationships, reduce the risk of addiction, strengthen your immune system, reduce the risk of infection, help you recover faster after illness, and help you become more creative and capable of making better decisions. Gratitude is like a Swiss pocketknife—a reliable tool you can always count on.

I take Leah's hand and say, "I am so incredibly grateful to have you as my daughter. I'm grateful that I've had the chance to be here with you these last seven blessed days and get to know you better. We walked together, talked, laughed, cried, visited a café, went to the cinema, and had a great time together. I am also so grateful that I can give you tools and strategies to help you build more resilience, inner strength, courage, and hope so that you can face the unknown and whatever life has in store for you each day. Like the ocean, each day is a gift. Sometimes gifts come wrapped in seemly incurable conditions or pain, loss, disappointments, fear, and tears. But remember the lotus flower. It's big, beautiful, and fragrant, and it blooms best when it grows from dirt and muck. I love you, Leah!"

Seven months later, a lot has changed in Leah's life. First and foremost, her mindset is resilient. She has gone from a fixed and primitive perspective to one of resilience characterized by growth, curiosity, and joy. From being skeptical, negative, and pessimistic on her behalf as she was in the initial phase, she is today more optimistic and constructive. She looks for opportunities and potential in the challenges she faces in everyday life.

She has moments of sadness and grief, but it is gratifying that she spends less and less time in states of despair, misery, and unhappiness. I don't want to say that it is neither my nor her mother's merit that Leah has managed to recover so well through the setback she has been through; Leah has had our full support in the process, but she has taken the challenges that have come and taken the steps herself. We have been close when she has needed us but have avoided the temptation to do the work for her.

The setbacks she has been through have clearly led to her growth as a person. Besides the fact that she has done well at school, she has taken care of an extra job at a local cafe. She has completed and passed the hunter's test, so she will go hunting for the first time in the autumn. At the time of writing, she has also achieved her goal of coming into a high-hanging aquaculture line at a high school on Froya, located at the coast in central Norway, where the opportunities to get a meaningful job after graduation are great.

We know now, from recent advances in neuroscience, that the capacity for resilience is innate in the brain, hardwired by evolution. And how well resilience develops as we mature depends on our life experiences and how those experiences shape the neural circuits and functioning of our brains. How quickly, adaptively, and effectively we can bounce back from terrible setbacks depends on our learned patterns of response to events and people. So, what we learn and pick up from our family, teachers, and coaches at an early age is encoded into our neural circuits and tends to become our behavior. But fortunately, what we have learned can also be unlearned.

The best arena for learning and personal development lies in the face of adversity, difficulties, disappointments, setbacks, and even disasters. But you don't understand that until you meet the experience, until you are present in it, feel the discomfort, the suffering, the fear of failing, the fear you don't have what it takes to get through the ordeal. But you can do it. Better than you know. It's like learning to play the piano; you don't play Beethoven on the first try. You first learn the scale, then simple melodies, and eventually you can advance to classical masterpieces by Mozart, Bach, or Beethoven.

The moment in front of you will sometimes (from time to time) contain waves of anxiety or stress or fear that wash through you—but never forget: "You are the ocean that includes all kinds of waves—you are neither defined nor restricted by them."

"Resilience isn't a single skill. It's a variety of skills and coping mechanisms. To bounce back from bumps in the road as well as failures, you should focus on emphasizing the positives."

~ Jean Chatzky

CHAPTER THREE

Learning to Ride the Waves & Storms of Life

By Kirsten Heynisch

"I am not afraid of storms, for I am learning how to sail my ship."
- Louisa May Alcott

A Broken Home

A broken heart and a lost home were the beginning of my journey of creating resilience—here is my story.

I just turned forty. I was mournfully musing on a plane from Leipzig to London, "Where is home? Is it a country, a place, a relationship?" A saying came to mind: "Your home is where your heart is." My heart was broken. The place I had considered my home had fallen apart. My sense of belonging was on shaky ground.

I grew up in East Germany and migrated to England when I was thirty to make a living and build a home with Jack. Moving country was a big turning point in my life, and my marriage had become my home for almost fifteen years. The end of my life with Jack shook me to my core.

The pilot requested everyone to have their seatbelt fastened, as the plane had hit some unexpected turbulence. The person next to me and I looked at each other with some trepidation, and she whispered, "This feels like a rollercoaster ride."

I nodded with a heavy-hearted sigh. "It really does."

I felt tears welling up inside. "If there is a God out there, please hear me; I don't think I can take any more rollercoaster rides." I felt exhausted and scared. I hadn't slept for months, feeling unsettled and overwhelmed by the emotional turbulence that the end of my marriage had stirred up in me.

While the plane felt as if it were shaking from side to side, I tried to read my book. In it, I encountered Jung's concept of God, which truly struck a chord. He describes God as reality itself: *"To this day God is the name by which I designate all things which cross my willful path violently and recklessly, all things which upset my subjective views, plans and intentions and change the course of my life for better or worse.*" I found comfort in this bold concept of God—I felt that my life, plans, and intentions had been violently and recklessly shaken up. Jung's understanding of God evoked a feeling of hope in me that there could be a deeper meaning in this painful experience.

My husband had left a few months ago and walked right into a relationship with a hot young babe with a high sex drive. What a cliché and a humiliating experience to be dumped in this way. Instead of holding my head high, I felt lost, raw, shattered, and betrayed.

Some morbid thinking crossed my mind and felt so real: "If this plane were to crash, it wouldn't be so bad. Go on, crash; I am ready!"

To the outside world, I was a high-powered, successful psychologist with many opportunities, resources, and gifts. I had just been promoted to set up and co-lead a team of clinicians supporting the most vulnerable and traumatized patients in the geographical area surrounding our clinic. On the inside, though, my world had fallen apart. I fell into a great blackness, feeling ashamed, alone, and deeply bereft.

Having supported and guided hundreds of traumatized, lost, hurt, and hopeless souls through their inner darkness, I now was the one wanting to give up. After I visited Germany, I went straight to my therapy session. I was crying and lamenting over the loss of my husband, the regrets I had, the baby we didn't have, and the life and companion I had lost. There was sincerity and a deep sorrow in my pain. I had truly and deeply loved and lost.

At some point, my therapist gently said, "You know, you have lost your marriage, not your life?"

The voice in my head was protesting: "So, what? I don't want *this* life."

The experience of separation had pulled me into a swamp, and I didn't know how to get out of it. At times, I felt I was going under. Nothing meant anything to me during this period.

After many months, tears, and therapy sessions, I began to understand that something internal to me had prolonged my suffering. What was it?

With the benefit of hindsight, I now understand that the new life circumstances required me to strengthen and flex my resilience muscle. Metaphorically speaking, I was on my knees and didn't know how to get up. I didn't know how to let go of my deep heartache, hurt, anger, shame, and sense of betrayal. Acceptance and peace of mind seemed out of reach.

Being a seeker at heart, my inner turmoil and emotional pain catalyzed me to go on a quest to learn about resilience and develop it. My passion for psychology, coaching, learning, and teaching inspired me to strengthen my resilience muscle and support and guide my clients to develop and leverage this inner core strength in their lives.

In the years that followed, I went on a self-assigned mission and adventure to build the foundations of resilience. If you are interested in the lessons I learned, keep reading.

In the following sections, I will share with you the birthplace of resilience, what resilience is, what it isn't, and the core ingredients that make up the recipe for creating resilience.

The Birthplace of Resilience

With the unrecoverable breakdown of my relationship, and during the years that followed, life pushed me to understand and accept that the nature of life is such that it is full of challenges, small and big. Life can be challenging, demanding, unfair, and simply a bitch.

And here is where resilience comes in. It takes resilience to get up and deal with these experiences and our vulnerabilities, whatever they are. The truth is we can't avoid challenges. There is a saying that goes, *We can't stop the waves, but we can learn to surf.*

In the years following my divorce, I was determined to learn to surf the waves and ride the storms of life. I fell off the surfboard many times. Sometimes, it felt like I was drowning, but I never did. I allowed life to teach me invaluable lessons that were core to becoming more aware, mature, and balanced—in essence, more resilient.

What Resilience Isn't

Some equate resilience with being tough and emotionally unaffected by difficult and hurtful experiences, believing we need to "toughen up." This is a huge misunderstanding. Being resilient doesn't mean we don't experience stress, vulnerability, helplessness, hurt, heartbreak, pain, loneliness, anger, and sadness.

When we are resilient, we can tolerate and work through emotional pain and suffering, rather than being stoical and emotionally unaffected.

It is true to say that a tough and unfeeling stance in the face of life's challenges, disappointments, and adversities most likely leads to depression and other emotional or physical difficulties somewhere down the line—or, at the very least, an inner dullness, numbness, and emptiness. I have seen it many times.

https://www.shutterstock.com/image-illustration/human-walking-rainbow-road-abstract-watercolor-1125560345

What Is Resilience?

True resilience is about our capacity to feel, experience, think about, deal with, process, work through, and recover from difficult life events and the vulnerabilities that are unearthed in the process. Resilience is about being on our knees and figuring out how to get up.

Life has a habit of pushing us out of our comfort zone. In my life, I have found myself repeatedly in places where I felt out of my depth, not knowing initially how to navigate the new territory.

My challenges were experiences many of us tend to face at some point in our life, such as the painful loss of a loving relationship, new challenging job roles, parenthood, the uncomfortable tension between being a devoted mother and loving my work, co-parenting, illness, and dating—just to name a few. These challenges are individual but also universal. Many of us are faced with learning to navigate the landscape of similar experiences.

What helped me was that every time I have faced a challenge, I accepted it as an opportunity to learn something about my way of responding to these challenges—some responses were helpful, others not.

In the process of cultivating acceptance and an openness to learning, I gradually discovered a core strength and an inner knowing that I can deal with the challenges and pains of life.

"*The turning point in the process of growing up is when you discover the core strength within you that survives all hurt.*"
- *Max Lerner*

This inner strength is resilience, which, if well developed, allows us to be with the emotional heights and depths of our lives.

In the following sections, I will share the key ingredients and foundations of creating resilience. I also want to express caution: cultivating resilience is not for the faint-hearted. It takes time, trial and error, perseverance, and courage.

Don't expect it to be easy. When you persevere, it will be deeply gratifying.

Self-Awareness

Self-awareness is the starting point of creating resilience (please see illustration).

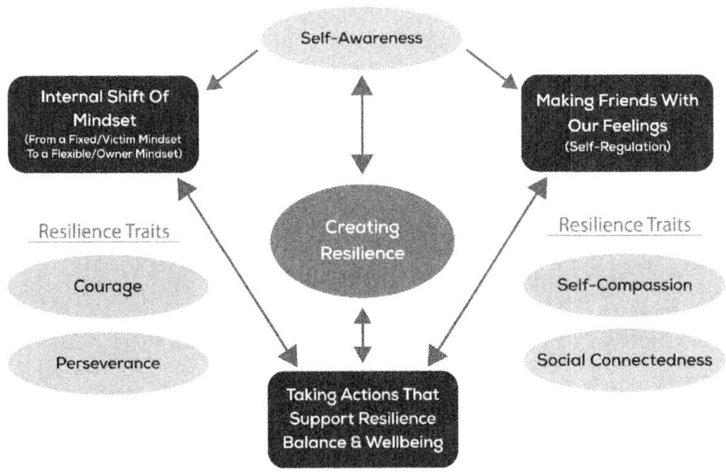

At the core of self-awareness is our ability to self-reflect and introspect, which helps us create conscious access to our inner world of thoughts, desires, intentions, feelings, and values.

Only when we are fully aware of our values, needs, thoughts, feelings, behaviors, strengths, and vulnerabilities can we understand, manage, direct, and communicate them in a helpful and life-enhancing way.

Self-awareness is a powerful tool and a vital steppingstone in creating resilience. Self-awareness can be likened to a beam of consciousness that can shine into our inner world of thoughts and feelings.

This beam of consciousness helps us see our inner demons, as well as our self-limiting and victim-based thought patterns and beliefs. This is a vital prerequisite to evolving our often-outdated mindset and developing a more resilient frame of mind.

The first step in creating good self-awareness is cultivating a sense of curiosity toward our inner experiences. In other words, self-awareness is supported and achieved by a movement inwards—by turning our focus and attention towards our inner world of thoughts, feelings, intentions, desires, and ambitions, just to name a few elements of our rich inner life.

Psychological therapy, journaling, or keeping a notebook are great ways to pay attention to what is going on in our inner world.

Self-awareness helps us recognize thinking patterns, perceptions, and emotional responses that can support or undermine our resilience.

Often, these mental states can be outside of our conscious awareness; however, with introspection and self-reflection, they will rise into consciousness, and with this, they become available to think about, work with, re-direct, and transform.

Experimenting with Emotional Skills Which Strengthen Resilience:

In your own practice of developing the emotional skill of self-awareness, you can use these reflective questions:

What did I do well today on my journey of creating resilience?
What challenges did I face?
What was I feeling?
How did I respond?
In retrospect, would I have responded differently?
What can I learn from this?
What is my intention for tomorrow?

Evolving a Flexible & Resilient Mindset

Our mindset is a complex tapestry shaped by our learned attitudes, beliefs, internalized values, behaviors, and emotional responses that have been shaped and conditioned in our childhood and teenage years by our family culture, which is a microcosm within the wider historical, political, and social context we grow up in.

Let's call this our conditioned mindset.

Our conditioned mindset shapes and colors how we make sense of the world and our experiences. In other words, our mindset is the lens through which we perceive and interpret life.

"We don't see things as they are, we see them as we are."
- Anais Nin

Not surprisingly, our mindset plays a pivotal role in coping with life's challenges.

Our mindset can support or undermine our resilience.

We tend to engage our conditioned mindset when we encounter tough times. As a result, we are pushed to make a much-needed internal mindset shift (please see illustration).

Here is an example from my life.

After my divorce, I developed increasing self-awareness about pockets of my mind that I would describe as hyper-critical, self-blaming, and shaming.

In the process of creating resilience, I realized that growing up behind the Berlin Wall in East Germany had fostered within me a mindset that was based on many destructive, self-limiting, and self-blaming ideas, attitudes, and belief systems.

I became aware that, in part, I felt victimized by the end of my marriage. I viewed this experience as a shameful and catastrophic failure on my part. In short, I was stuck in a passive, powerless, and highly judgmental mindset—not a fun place to live in; in fact, it caused unhappiness and undermined my resilience.

It became clear to me that I needed to dismantle my conditioned mindset. So, as a result, I began to diligently deconstruct my inner Berlin Walls (old, conditioned mindset) and sculpt my new mindset, which was much more flexible, supportive, kind, forgiving, and resilient. A much more light-hearted, safe, and loving place to reside in.

The truth is that we can blame ourselves, our partners, our past or circumstances, and our managers, and the list is endless. But have you noticed that blaming keeps us stuck? Blaming others and ourselves gets in the way of creating resilience.

The Good News About Shifting Our Mindset

The exciting discovery of modern neuroscience supports the possibility of changing our mindset. Neuroscience clearly highlights that our brain has the flexibility to create new patterns of response to life events—throughout our entire life. This is wonderful news for building resilience.

Let me illustrate this with some of my own life experiences.

From a Fixed/Passive/Victim Mindset to a Flexible/Resilient/ Owner Mindset

Life behind the Berlin Wall greatly impacted my childhood and teenage years. Growing up in an oppressive political and cultural system imposed spoken and unspoken expectations of undue acquiescence and compliance without protest.

A rebel and free spirit at heart, family and cultural expectations squashed my authentic self-expression, aliveness, and playfulness.

Within the family and at school, my natural and healthy need for self-expression and self-assertion was stifled. When I expressed anger in my family, which is a natural and necessary part of growing up and finding our voice, I was often met with strong disapproval and misunderstanding.

As a child and as a teenager, this was deeply hurtful. As a result, I became a compliant, good, and hardworking child, teenager, and young woman. I adapted to my family and cultural context by learning to shine through my achievements at school and university. This helped me feel liked, respected, and approved of by my parents, teachers, and peers while being alienated from my authentic emotional life. Within this context, I couldn't develop strong resilience in my younger years. I made up for it later in life.

As a young woman, I struggled with my conditioned mindset, prioritizing compliance over authenticity and resilience. I could easily feel like a "troublemaker" when I expressed disagreement, even when articulated in a very thoughtful and considerate way. I also found it hard to say no and set healthy boundaries in my relationships. This was a problem. I was stuck in my conditioned mindset.

If we remain tied to our conditioned mindset in our adult years, we genuinely are passive sufferers of our past. This understanding and awareness fueled my passion and motivation to create a mindset and inner stance that supports my growth, learning, creativity, and resilience.

This was not easy. At times, it felt like a heroic act and an inner revolution to outgrow my over-learned and outdated compliant and conditioned way of being.

Part of this was to step away from blame and shame and take responsibility for my feelings, choices, mood, health, and finances—no matter what. Creating a resilient mindset requires us to take full responsibility for every aspect of our lives, including every thought and feeling.

Victor Frankl beautifully highlights this in his book *Man's Search for Meaning*: "Between stimulus and response, there is a space. In that space is our power to choose our response. In our response lies our growth and our freedom."

The bottom line is this: We can't always choose what happens to us, but we can consider, reflect, and choose how we respond to what comes our way. When we learn to inhabit this space between what happens (external circumstances) and our response to it, we begin to embody and own our inner authority and resilience.

This way of taking ownership for our feelings, experiences, and decisions is at the heart of a resilient mindset. It requires an internal shift from our conditioned mindset, which tends to be a rather passive, inflexible, victim-based mindset, into a more flexible, owner-based growth mindset (please see illustration).

Why is this so important? Our conditioned reactions and mental filters tend to shrink our vision to the narrow range of past experiences in our younger years. On the other hand, a resilient mindset has a much wider and more expansive perspective, which supports creative problem-solving, fosters improved social connections, and increases clarity of mind.

Even though hard-won, the reward of creating a resilient mindset has been unexpected and wonderful for me: I have become more light-hearted, flexible, able to bend and twist with life, and more accepting of what is—rather than wishing things, people, and life to be different. In this way, my life has become more fun, playful, creative, and enjoyable.

Experimenting with Emotional Skills Which Strengthen Resilience:

I encourage you to pause and be curious about the following reflective questions pertaining to your mindset:

In what cultural and social context was your mindset shaped?
Is your current mindset still serving you or is it hindering you in dealing with your current challenges?
What internal shift in mindset would you benefit from?

Making Friends with Our Feelings—Self-Regulation

Another crucial ingredient and emotional skillset in creating resilience is making friends with our childhood wounds, feelings, and vulnerabilities (please see illustration).

Why is this important?

We all know that experiencing feelings is core to being human. We also know that our emotions can get intense and turbulent at times.

The real challenge in creating resilience is to contain innumerable experiences throughout our lives with all their emotional heights and depths.

This includes painful experiences, such as loss, heartbreak, grief, disappointment, loneliness, anger, and other vulnerable feelings on the broad and nuanced spectrum of human emotions.

It is vital to understand that we cannot selectively numb emotions. When avoiding, disconnecting from, and numbing uncomfortable and painful feelings, we inevitably numb our capacity to feel joy, love, inspiration, creativity, happiness, compassion, and gratitude.

In my quest to learn about resilience, I understood that life's experiences and challenges are unmanageable and overwhelming to the degree that we cannot tolerate and manage the feelings that are evoked within us. The potential range of experiences stretches from being open to the beauty of nature, compassion, and love for another to an awareness of our limitations and brokenness, the pains and joys of love and life, conflict, isolation, and disintegration, as well as integration and harmony.

Feeling the uncomfortable, raw, and vulnerable feelings is a real challenge for many of us. Most of us grew up in families and cultures where the powerful myth that vulnerability is a weakness and a flaw permeated people's thinking.

As a result, many of us have come to reject and defend against our vulnerability, which we often associate with emotions like anxiety, fear, shame, grief, sadness, anger, and disappointment—feelings we often aren't comfortable with and don't easily talk about, even when they profoundly affect our well-being and our relationships.

In my younger years, I struggled immensely with regulating some of my emotions. It's been a big part of creating resilience to understand, accept, respect, nurture, articulate, and manage the emotional parts of my being.

Learning to manage and stabilize our feelings, rather than let them hijack us or shut us down, is the practice of developing emotional regulation. Self-regulation and resilience are closely related.

It is helpful to understand that our emotions are signals that require our attention. Making friends with our feelings is about learning to skillfully attend to, experience, understand, and accept our feelings and decide what life-supporting actions to take in the service of good self-regulation.

Taking Actions that Support Resilience

Psychological research helps us understand that emotions are signals and catalysts for behaviors and actions. Ideally, our actions and behaviors will support our sense of safety, well-being, growth, and resilience.

Resilience is supported by taking life-supporting and life-enhancing actions.

For example, the experience of loneliness after my break-up was a signal that I needed to grow my social connections. I acted on this signal in various ways, and through trial and error, I gradually managed to create a supportive and stimulating social network around me.

This didn't happen overnight—step by step, I took actions that supported the creation of a more fulfilling sense of social connectedness, which is closely associated with resilience.

I experimented with various ideas. Some worked, others didn't. I tried internet dating, which I didn't enjoy at the time. I learned cooking and invited friends for meals, which was nurturing and mutually enjoyable.

Carefully considered and heart-centered actions of all sorts gradually helped me build new and meaningful connections with like-minded people. This approach also guided me to the opportunity to meet one of my romantic partners, which was a healing, supportive, and uplifting experience at the time.

In my quest to understand and create resilience, I realized that building inner strength is a dynamic process that engages our whole being—feelings, thinking, and actions.

Experimenting with Emotional Skills Which Strengthen Resilience:

What actions would support you in building and flexing your resilience muscle?
What would you consider life-supporting and life-enhancing choices and actions in your current circumstances?

Social Connectivity

With the end of my marriage, the most central and intimate bond I had developed with another human being was suddenly unavailable. I lost my best friend and the person with whom I had shared a home, a bed, and a table for many years. That was hard. Feelings of loneliness, isolation, and a lack of belonging became my new companions for some time.

In response to this experience, I have made thoughtful and solid choices and took decisive actions to increase my social connectivity and create new meaning and purpose. For example, I invested a lot of time, money, and energy in pursuing a five-year training course in group psychotherapy. Part of the training requirements was to join a psychotherapy group throughout the training. I stayed in this hugely supportive, reflective, and insightful therapy group for six years.

My therapy group helped me process, heal, and overcome childhood trauma, repair my inner foundations, transcend my sense of betrayal and disappointment, and gradually let go of my heartbreak, sorrow, and remorse. During these years, I increasingly understood that being resilient is a process that takes time, perseverance, and a willingness to flex and bend with life and what it brings to us—wanted and unwanted.

The social context of this lengthy training program became a place where I could exercise my social resilience muscle. It helped me feel much more at ease in groups, which is most of the time, given that we spend much of our time in groups. I will always fondly remember this place, which felt like home, and the meaningful connections I have made there.

One of the many rewards of this training course were that it had earned me the privilege to support and facilitate my clients' social resilience muscle within the therapy groups I have been running since.

Experimenting with Emotional Skills Which Strengthen Resilience:

I encourage you to reflect on your current social context—what is working for you, and what isn't?
If you don't currently feel embedded enough in a supportive social context, what actions could you take to create improved social connectivity?

Choosing Courage over Comfort

Becoming comfortable with the uncomfortable is a fundamental part of creating resilience (please see illustration).

Resilience demands us to leave our comfort zone.

The many challenges and milestones in my life—migrating from Germany to the UK, establishing myself as a psychologist in another country, divorce, the tightrope of being a devoted mother and successful professional, and co-parenting—pushed me into hugely uncomfortable places.

I had to continually step into the discomfort of forging my path beyond the conditioned expectations which I and maybe others had in mind.

Creating resilience takes courage and tenacity. When we dare to step out of our powerless childhood conditioning, we often experience huge discomfort and, at times, overwhelming anxiety.

The good news is that as competent, coping adults, we can learn to manage our anxious and uncomfortable feelings, speak our minds, and negotiate our relationships.

In this sense, creating resilience can be scary and liberating simultaneously—it is a choice and an act of courage in the face of our childhood conditioning. The pull of staying small and dependent can be strong and seductive.

I became aware of this, especially in the years after my divorce, when I was still in part hoping for an external rescue mission—a fantasy that someone out there would spare me the often uncomfortable and turbulent experiences in life. A part of me still wished and hoped for protection and rescue, maybe by my ex-husband and possibly the arrival of a new partner.

While I did meet new partners, I had to face the truth that I, and only I, could reach into the depths of my soul and find the sparks of life that resided there. By reaching into that core place, I found the honesty, commitment, love, and courage to directly meet my anxiety and sorrow, loneliness, and lostness—all of it—and take full responsibility for my life.

Initially, I experienced this responsibility as an unwanted burden, something unjust, an insurmountable problem, a bad joke that life and the universe had played on me. Robert Frost's quote speaks to this sense of betrayal and disillusionment: "*Forgive, O Lord, my little jokes on Thee, and I'll forgive Thy the great big joke on me.*"

Over time, I began to feel the liberating and at times exhilarating force that comes with the territory of choosing courage over comfort—and almost getting comfortable in that place.

Perseverance and Struggle in the Process of Creating Resilience

What helped me enormously on my path of creating resilience is the understanding that struggle has purpose and meaning. We all have our struggles, our dark places—whether we talk about them or not.

Human struggles are personal and universal at the same time. Struggle and adversity are often the birthplaces of building inner resources, resilience, and fortitude.

With the divorce, my map of reality had changed, and to my dismay, the years and experiences that followed continued to be off the map. A year after my marriage ended, I started a new relationship, and a few years later, I had a baby. Being a mother has been one of my life's most fulfilling gifts and experiences. Like being a psychologist, motherhood has offered me enjoyment, fulfillment, meaning, purpose, and direction in life.

However, life had further challenges in store. I faced the heart-sinking reality that I was not in a sustainable relationship with my baby's father. I made the agonizingly difficult decision to end the relationship, which involved negotiating co-parenting arrangements—another momentous task I didn't feel prepared for, and another chance to create resilience.

These unsettling years of my life appeared to never end. In these years, my perseverance was tested, and my tenacity was strengthened. Uncertainty and doubt were my companions and only constant. In these years, I learned that enormous creative potential is brought to life through our struggles and challenges. It is the grit that makes the pearls of wisdom and creates resilience.

The Parable of the Moth beautifully illustrates this:

The Parable of the Moth

"A man found the cocoon of an emperor moth. He took it home to watch the moth hatch. On that day, a small opening appeared. He sat and watched the moth struggle for several hours to force its body through the tiny hole. Then the moth stopped as if it had gotten as far as it could and could go no further.

In his kindness, the man decided to help, so he took a pair of scissors and snipped off the remaining bit of cocoon. The moth emerged easily but had a swollen body and small, shriveled wings.

The man continued to watch the moth, expecting at any moment the wings would enlarge and expand to help support its body. Neither happened, and the little moth spent the rest of its short life crawling around with a swollen body and shriveled legs. It was never able to fly.

In his kindness and haste, the man did not understand that struggling to get out of the cocoon was the only way to force fluid from the body into the moth's wings. Freedom and flight would only come after the struggle. By depriving the moth of a struggle, the man deprived the moth of life."
(Unknown author)

I love this story. It beautifully highlights that struggle and perseverance are vital in developing our wings and being able to take off and fly—which is essentially what resilience is. The Parable of the Moth also poignantly emphasizes that there are no shortcuts.

While there are no shortcuts, there is deep value in our life's struggles. Freedom and flight only come after the struggle. Through our struggles, we become resilient and free, stronger than ever before, ready to face the next challenge.

Self-Compassion and Resilience

Looking back on my journey of creating resilience, self-compassion has been one of my strongest allies.

I feel profound gratitude for a handful of significant and supportive companions on my journey: my deeply attuned psychotherapist, who nurtured the unformed in me over the years, my therapy group, my life partners, family, and friends. Alongside the support and connection with others, I discovered the value and necessity of self-compassion.

Self-compassion is another fundamental resilience trait (please have a look at the illustration for the four resilience traits).

Over the years, I managed to cultivate a deep love and respect for the young girl and woman I once was and the woman I am continuously in the process of becoming.

https://www.shutterstock.com/image-illustration
/human-love-spirit-powerful-energy-connect-1097462351

Self-compassion helped me to become more comfortable with solitude. The process of creating resilience can, at times, be a very solitary journey, and self-compassion and solitude are good companions.

In fact, I learned to value and enjoy solitude and feel replenished by spending time by myself and with myself.

Self-compassion supported me in learning to live with the questions, embrace uncertainty, and accept all that is unresolved in my heart without forcing the answers.

With increasing resilience and self-compassion, I have become less fearful and more daring. I also understand more deeply that life truly is what we make of it.

I learned to accept that no one is coming to save me, not because the world is a mean place, but simply because no one else can.

Experimenting with Emotional Skills Which Strengthen Resilience:

I encourage you to pause and be curious about some of your life's struggles.

What supported you through these challenges? What life lessons did you learn in the process?

My Journey Is My Home

To come full circle, thinking back to my younger self sitting on the plane from Germany to England, pondering what home means, I have discovered that *my journey is my home.*

I have understood that my home is not a place, a country, or a relationship. While relationships and places can be deeply meaningful, my truest home is my path through life, and my most faithful companion is resilience.

Good resilience allows us to heal, to deal with and bounce back from life's most challenging experiences—it can carry us through life and the dark places more than any other skillset. Resilience is a superpower that can be developed and strengthened throughout our lives.

My journey of creating resilience has enabled me to claim my life and take responsibility for the fullest expression of who I want to be and become. And from this new vantage point, I now understood that yes, I had lost my marriage, but not my life—my life is here for the living, loving, and co-creating.

Each of us has been given a life, and we are responsible for the fullest expression of what wants to be lived through us.

Creating resilience necessitates continual choice—stepping away from destructive and life-inhibiting aspects of our being and stepping towards new and life-giving possibilities.

For me, creating resilience has been a profoundly soulful path from feeling broken to feeling whole. I know that this is possible for you too. I wish you well on your journey of creating resilience—a superpower and one of the most faithful life companions you will ever find.

"Resilience is not just for surviving the worst day of your life, it's for thriving every day of your life."

~ Dr. Rick Hanson

CHAPTER FOUR

My Grief is No Longer my Dark Weakness

By Diana Elena Matei

As I looked into his sapphire eyes, I saw the light within dimming. I held his hand for a moment and then it felt as though his last breath escaped his physical body. I placed my hand under his nose and screamed at my heavily pregnant mother that my brother was not breathing. We called for assistance and a slow-motion scene began developing in front of me: the nurse barely walking toward our salon, a scream from across the hall, and the tray behind me falling and releasing the contents of a small bottle of sanitizer. As soon as she saw my brother, I was asked in a high-pitched voice to leave as she pushed the alert button. I was thrown out of the ward and sent home afraid.

On my way home, the thoughts I had kept at bay all day started flooding back into my already scattered and vulnerable mind. This was the beginning of my younger version making acquaintance with resilience, somehow unconsciously, back then. I was just starting to learn about what a resilient mindset was and how I could use it to further my growth, although the root emotion at the time was fear.

What if this time he will not make it? What if this time is going to be his last? What if all of this is my fault? Perhaps if I had told Mum that he threw up more than three times, maybe she would have taken him to the hospital earlier. Or she would have made some magic potion and cured him faster than those incompetent doctors.

However, I did not mention to her that he puked his soul out more than three times because she looked so tired, and also stressed out after another meeting with the teachers right before the new school year. And with everything going on with the divorce to top it all, I just thought that I did not want to add any more stress to the pile. My mum is one of the most resilient women I know; nonetheless, she was at a tipping point, and Andru has always recovered quickly from pretty much anything. But this time, he vomited more times than I could count. And something felt wrong. And I reassured my mum that everything was going to be alright because he only threw up three times, no more. Yet, this morning, Nicky, my second sister, had found him convulsing and woke Mum up, who then called the ambulance straight away. She told the people in charge that he had eaten wild mushrooms and plums and that he needed some milk and stomach cleansing. One of them simply shoved the pregnant woman aside, looking at her with a certain superiority and asking her if she had finished her medical degree and knew better than them. Although Mum tried to say that her intuition never fails her, he threw a few more derogatory remarks at her, reminding her that he was more qualified than an English teacher and finally took off with her son.

Before afternoon arrived, my little brother was misdiagnosed at least three times as having encephalitis, then hepatitis, then HIV. They did two tomography scans and took a few more blood samples. At around 1 PM, the doctor came furiously at my mum, demanding she justify herself as to why she did not mention the food he had ingested so they could pump some fluids into his stomach to cleanse it. With incredible patience and understanding for the medic, as he had a long shift, Mum said, "I did. You never listened. I just want my little boy to be healthy again because he is looking forward to playing with his baby brother due in two months." My incredible mum always demonstrated compassion, even under duress, because of her resilient mindset, as she spoke her desires into existence.

Andru has been hospitalized before, and we knew we had to provide the extra money for the staff to do pretty much anything. I was always disgusted with how everything in Romania goes with a side dish of bribe in every field. I have always blamed the politicians leading our country towards the economic hole we are in as a nation, because if the money had been managed and distributed properly while the people had been prioritized, then bribes would not be a "go-to" tool every single time some wheels needed greasing to move better, faster. It took me almost two decades to reframe my thinking around circumstances that are outside my control and to focus on my inner world, the only one I am in control of and the center of my resilience.

This illusion of being in control of everything around me (also called my own Houdini Mental Show because I thought I could BE the change, but I didn't know what the change should be) is what gave me the nudge into creating resilience in my life, under different circumstances.

Mihai, my mum's partner, and the father of the next three, most incredible siblings, pulled together some money and paid the nurses to ensure that they treated my brother with utmost care.

At that time, we were experiencing a financial crisis as a family. Our main dish for breakfast, lunch, and supper was bread and butter with a pinch of salt, and sometimes tomatoes during those very hot summer days. Hence, we went foraging as we lived near the hills that would lead into woods where we would get hazelnuts, plums, mushrooms and so much more, depending on the season. Mother Nature has been good to us. That financial situation impacted each of us differently. I liked it until I didn't, but that was the menu for a while, and the options were that limited. I created my own trauma and made an oath to myself that I would never allow this to happen to myself or to my future children. Never again. For Ana, my second sister, this left a certain scar and fear of never having enough, so she'd always push until she was sure there was nothing left. Nicky, the most resilient of us all, pushed until she healed her money wounds and created her own empire based on wellness and health.

As I entered our apartment, I went straight for the bed and started praying, hoping for the best. At midnight, Mihai woke me up to go a few blocks back and ask Dad to run to the hospital to donate blood so they could save my brother. As I returned, I could smell the liquor on his breath when he asked me, "Are you ready for the big bomb?" And in that moment, I knew Andru was no longer a part of our world. I muffled my screams with a pillow after breaking everything breakable nearby. When my mum came in minutes later, barely breathing, I started screaming from the top of my lungs at her while looking at her bump. "If this baby boy wants to die, he can die now! I do not want to meet him just so he can die afterward!"

She held me in her warm embrace while allowing my grief to manifest, as she kept hers at bay for our sakes. That night, I stopped praying. Andru would not let me go to sleep before I would say my prayers so he could repeat after me, but he was not here now. And God ceased existing for me. I didn't know how to pray any longer. For the first time, I was forced to go within.

I started creating my own kind of resilience, as I felt like I had only been surviving for a very long time, not living. I misunderstood the two terms "surviving" and "living" as being synonyms and I was not aware of it, but I thought that I deserved whatever was thrown at me. I believed that, eventually, someone would read my mind, understand my grief, and fix my broken heart since I felt unable to do that myself.

When they moved his body into the chapel, I could not stop staring. He looked like a teenager despite dying at only two years, nine months, one week, and six days. Somehow, it felt like he was sleeping, but I knew better as three years earlier, I felt the same powerlessness upon my grandma's passing.

Only this time, my guilt and shame were the ones keeping me warm.

When I saw the coffin being lowered into the freshly dug hole in which he would sleep forever, my faith was buried with him, and my anger started eating whatever was left of my soul. Seeing people smiling at me or laughing on the street as I was walking, I felt an explosion of anger misdirected to anything and anyone.

How could God take back his angel when we needed him more? That meant there is no God as He would not put his Creation through so much pain and suffering. Or would He? Maybe He enjoys people's grief because so many deny its existence. How can everyone be so relaxed when my brother will soon experience oblivion? All these people, are they unaware of the fact that my little brother is no more? Why is this happening? Why have I not done something, as I was the eldest sister, and it was my responsibility? My disempowering thoughts were eroding my resilient nature and soon became a part of my personality.

I should have known better.

These deep regrets were being carved into my soul.

The questions kept me wandering in the darkness for over a decade, a time in which I was bullied, I moved schools, universities, cities, and countries, I experienced racism and bias at my work, and I tasted the bitterness of betrayal as my trust in certain relationships was broken. Yet, despite this, I have never prayed for better, because I felt I deserved it all. There was nothing after we died, so what was the point in even trying to believe in anything?

But there was! There was so much more to be, do, and have faith in! Little did I know that this time of adversity would be my steppingstone to developing resilience. It was like a muscle awaiting its workout.

The three little siblings born after Andru became my rays of hope, my raison d'être. I promised myself that they would not experience poverty. They became my source of resilience. After their father had left them for a well-known person whose financial situation he craved, perhaps to fill that empty space within, I promised myself I was going to do a better job at being a big sister for all of them. I went to study and work abroad, and I sent money home monthly for whatever was needed.

I recall that one morning, I wanted to call my workplace so that I may be late and noticed I had a 43-minute call with Mum. I did not remember that call taking place the previous night after a bottle of Baileys. It was my first experience of getting so drunk that I could not even fully recall a conversation with her. I called Mum to ask what we talked about, as I may have said things that I did not mean, and as always, she briefly said: "You would have never opened up otherwise, so thank you for being yourself during that call and sharing all that with me, darling."

I was in shock as I was used to bottling up my emotions, not really sharing them and I got mad at myself for putting my own mum through that. I never opened up about myself as much after Andru's ascension, and despite my mum's countless methods and attempts to talk with me about it, she mostly allowed me the time and space to heal, trusting that when I was ready to talk with her about it in depth, I would.

My coping mechanism was to push myself to the limits and break them, eventually. My colorful style of poetry writing turned into a darker-than-black style, always highlighting the source of those lyrics: my uncontrollable grief and anger towards God. Listening to music was my first go-to tool every time I experienced strong emotions; when I was angry and I wanted to scream at people at which I could not, I would play rock songs at maximum volume until my ears rang in pain, all the while cleaning everything I could get my hands on.

When I would fall into the barrel of melancholy, I would start listening to music from my early teens and even earlier as it felt nostalgic, and I made that period 'my happy place.'I would sing my emotions out as I knew the lyrics by heart, and my voice could reach notes that I was not even aware of. When I succeeded in a competition, at school, at work, or anywhere else, I would listen to songs that would make me jump and dance with happiness and gratitude all around the house. Music was my resilience muscle during the aftershock of Andru's passing.

Upon beginning my meditation practice, I believed that everything resumed focusing on nothingness while sitting in the Lotus Position for hours in a row in silence or humming a mantra. I learned that meditation is for everyone who is ready and open. We may meditate while doing dishes, while visualizing, walking, writing and so much more. It's an experience that's unique to each of us. My monkey brain would not be quiet for a moment and always wander off onto the next task I had to do rather than focusing on visualizing myself as accomplished. When I finally realized I had the gift of leading meditations, I began building my resilience while working with my own limits. As limits are mainly self-imposed, resilience was a word I was using because I thought it was *cool*. Hence, creating it took much longer than anticipated. As a matter of fact, I now know it's an ongoing process as new challenges arise every single day in our lives, encouraging each of us to keep on building resilience.

After I finished my studies in Denmark, I had a powerful conversation about togetherness with Ana and Nicky, my sisters from my mum's first marriage, and I decided to move to the UK so that we could work hard, sell the apartment from Romania, and pay the debts that kept on burying Mum under a lot of stress. After that, we would move everyone to the UK, buy a house together, and finally a toast to our "happily ever after" as a family. The three of us rented a house, Dad showed up shortly after, and a new chapter of trials and errors began.

I fell in love with my Twin Flame, Julian (aka J). It was truly love at first sight. Although I met him a year before, while visiting Ana, he was in a relationship back then, and I stated that I did not want to become "that kind of woman". As soon as I came back, he contacted me again and we decided to give it a chance "to whatever this was". We were 180 degrees different, and although we never had a fight, we both concealed our emotional and mental wounds with a lack of deep communication.

Nobody gave us more than a year together and yet, here we are, nine years later, growing stronger than ever before, supporting each other's growth. Was it easy? Certainly not. There were moments when we disagreed a lot on so many things. Living with some of my family members for so long was rather challenging for our relationship for different reasons. We all had different living standards. Sometimes, it felt like I was imposing on what was to be done and when because I felt best when everything had an order. Chaos scared me as I would associate it with uncertainty and lack of control. Pushing through these difficult times strengthens our bond and resilience to overcome challenges together.

Furthermore, J was born in a very traditional family where everything ran on the old, outdated programming, while I was blessed with parents that were more modern, spiritual, and open to all the possibilities the Divine had to offer. He moved in after our first year together, and we both became more aware of each other's shadows. We had to work with ourselves for our relationship to grow and transform, every day a little bit more. J had been cheated on by almost every woman he had a relationship with before me, and he was easily triggered from a place of jealousy and possessiveness whenever I went out with my friends or travelled alone. I internalized those moments and then I reacted in a manner that matched his vibration. We learned through supporting each other's transformation of past wounds that we could expand the compassion and resilience of our relationship.

Moreover, after moving in, Dad kept on changing jobs and construction projects according to the highest bidders, while also keeping his gambling and gaming passions very much alive as a way to escape the reality he created for himself until then. Ana fell in love again after her first betrayal and experienced the same shortly after. She kept on moving in and out of the house and the children kept on being uprooted from the countless countries she travelled to. She could still not found herself. Both my parents and I took out loans to cover some of the debts that her latest partner, Antonio, left her with after running away with what my sister thought of as her best friend. This situation left a deep money wound to be healed for the years to come in our family and in my relationship.

The family dynamics changed when I asked Ana not to come over until I could heal or at least begin to and my dad stopped talking with me until I felt forced to get over it. That's when I underwent a deep healing through forgiveness as I kept on learning from each experience through the lens of resilience. I have also realized we all have our own timeline and so does my sister. Growth is built through healing and resilience and my sister is on her own path to create it.

Nicky fell in love and moved with her the man who is now her husband, Cristi, back in Romania where they opened *Human*, the first fitness clinic in the world with a personalized concept on 1:1 training, Kineto, and nutrition. They grew to be very successful and inspired me and J to work on our business concept as well.

My brother, Alex, came to study in London, and I realized there were plenty of scars he carried forth from feeling unloved by his dad when he was alive, and countless fears that grew further and faster after Mihai's death and reflected into the depression spiral which he kept on perpetuating for the past few years. ADHD was also playing an influential factor in all this because Alex usually gets self-motivated for a few days and then loses interest as he gets distracted by something else that could be 'his big breakthrough'. Currently, it feels like Alex has a lot of work on creating the resilience to push through difficult times.

Our dream of buying a house together, as a family, was not fulfilled and once again, another failure left me with a bitter taste. Although it felt like I took responsibility for every failure, be it my own or by my dear ones, I was always afraid of success, and I was not even aware of it until recently, because I did not understand that both failure and success are the result of your trials and errors. What matters the most is what you do with it afterwards. Both failure and success supported me in this healing journey while creating resilience and becoming the best version of myself.

One day, while visiting Claudia, one of my high-school besties, I saw her blessing a glass of water. I got frustrated at first and said, "Religion is the cause of all wars, I am not going to indulge that."

She only smiled and replied from a place of faith: "This past year I had an NDE and believe me, I am beyond grateful to be alive. It was God's will and I have faith that everything is going according to God's plan." A plant was seeded in that very moment as the faint memory of Mum always encouraging us to bless our food came forward.

Deep down, I always knew blessing the water, food, and everything else was a powerful tool to reclaim the magic within. My journey may seem like a breeze for some, and like a hurricane for others. For me, it was all about healing, learning from everything and everyone, and keeping the process of creating resilience ongoing.

My mum noticed I had begun blessing my food once again but said nothing. She patiently waited until I had finally outgrown my shadows and opened up slowly. While being caught in a job that provided comfortable earnings and pushed me towards my final burnout to date, I began learning and practicing holistic therapies, attended EFT events, got certified as an Angelic and Crystal Healer, became attuned as a Reiki Master, and gave intuitive readings. I also started my own podcast where I invite people to share their rock bottoms and the process they went through to shine their light unapologetically; and finally, I have found my Soul Purpose: intuitive coaching built on powerful transformation while creating resilience.

I am not yet a millionaire with two decades of coaching to support my current path. At the time of writing this, I am D. Intuitive Coach with over one thousand hours of intuitive coaching reflected in the transformational results of my very happy clients. I am always here and ready to serve those who are ready to take a deep dive within themselves via a plethora of methods and open to receiving all the possibilities available for their highest good. D. Intuitive Coach is not only a hat I wear with my clients, but an aspect of me, of my Self. I support women to reconnect with their Divine Self by allowing grief to manifest and release those emotional blocks that hold their mind and body hostage. Grieving does not make you weak and it is not a dark place that we can hide in the deepest corner of our being forever. What we perceive as the loss of a dear person, an aspect of Self, a relationship, a pet, a project, and so on can be harnessed into a new beginning as you create resilience, heal, and grow from it. Grieving is a journey that can be shared with those ready to listen from a place of love, compassion, and support. I am ready to listen. Are you ready to share? Creating a resilient mindset is the fertile ground that births transformation in every area of our lives.

Previously, I was not aware of the power of this word and how much transformation it encompasses. It's like a stress ball that keeps on being squeezed, pulled, shoved, and yet somehow it always retains its shape thanks to the multitude of actions that have been taken to create the space for transformation. One that is not visible at first. However, the more actions we take, the more visible the wrinkles get on the stress ball, thereby revealing how useful it was for the one exploiting it.

Resilience is created, we are not born with it. It is created through the conditioned mind as we learn to unlearn old patterns and relearn new programs to bounce back stronger than before. Bouncing back from the grief of losing my little brother was the hardest, longest, and most challenging way to recreate myself through resilience. I was not ready for a long time, and when I barely touched the handle of the door towards that part of my soul, all the guilt, shame, anger, and other fear-related emotions came running with a vengeance. Bottled up for far too long, they were ready to burst regardless of the methods I would have invoked. As soon as the door was ajar, I couldn't shut it any longer. I had to confront them face to face, this is how resilience is forged by confronting our challenges and rising inspired by them. Moreover, when I did that, I also built another step on the stairway towards a new version of myself vibrating on a higher frequency. Maintaining this frequency is what encourages me to create and conquer new levels of resilience.

Resilience has its own rhythm; it does not work on your imposed timeline. Sometimes it can take a day or two, sometimes a few months, and other times, it can take years. Unless you are ready to take the first step towards its creation, resilience has no true meaning for you as we all have our own unique experiences in this dimension and a timeline to fulfil our Soul Contract. We have our own lessons to learn and blessings to receive. We are all One, but here, we all have our unique light to shine.

My faith has been patiently waiting for me to heal by creating resilience, so I can shine my light unapologetically. And here I am today, sharing with you a fragment of my life, trusting that it is going to reach the ones that need to hear this the most in Divine

Timing, dear reader. Sometimes all we need to be inspired is a glimpse into someone else's life who has been through similar experiences to the ones in which we find ourselves.

You are not a victim of your past, but a powerful creator of your own life. The present is happening now, and tomorrow is not guaranteed. Take a leap of faith, believe in yourself, and trust the process as you create resilience through powerful transformations.

"Resilience is silent and deep,
like roots. It doesn't announce itself.
It doesn't explode outward.
It doesn't fall. It doesn't break.
It simply always is. And you are."

~ Victoria Erickson

CHAPTER FIVE

Developing Resilience After Trauma

By Corrina Carmen Andersen

I grew up in a dysfunctional environment believing life was a battle, and you had to fight for what you deserve. My creativity was built from resilience to failure, disappointment, and trauma.

My parents were relatively young when I was born, my father barely twenty years old, my mother twenty-one. We lived in a semi-detached house in the suburbs of inner Sydney and were lucky enough to have my grandmother live next door.

My mother was a young stay-at-home mom, and my father was an apprentice electrician working mandatory night shifts. My brother was born when I was four, and it wasn't long after that he went to live with my grandmother.

My mother drank a lot. There were times when I would find her unconscious on the living room floor and could not wake her up. I have memories where she often would disappear from the house without a word, so I repeated the same ritual of roaming up and down our small suburban streets in search of her. I asked neighbors and strangers, "Have you seen my mother?" Most often, the reply was, "What does your mother look like, dear?" As a wave of unease rushed over my body and into the deep pit of my stomach, I would begin to tremble. As my thoughts raced with fear of the unknown, I couldn't help but feel overwhelmed.

The repeated words that echoed in my mind became old and stale, and the feelings of anxiety and uncertainty became all too familiar. Knocking on doors and wandering up driveways from one end of the street to the other became exhausting. So often was my head down, my steps heavy, as I made my way from one end of the road to the other. I had no option but to turn around and wander back home. What followed were the overwhelming feelings of loneliness that soured into despair. Around this time, I began to escape into the safety of my mind and withdraw. Rather than be resilient and face her demons, I witnessed my mother turn to the bottle to escape her reality.

As my mother's drinking escalated, she became more erratic and volatile. I was often afraid to be alone with her, there was an uneasiness inside that often paralyzed me with fear. Instinctively, I felt unsafe, so it didn't take long for me to see her as the monster in my closet. Thinking back, it was psychologically quite complex. Despite my young age, and as challenging as the situation was, this experience did strengthen my inner resilience which would then help me face and overcome many adversities later in life.

During my adolescence and teenage years, I attended many AA meetings with my mum. This was not my choice and I felt incredibly uncomfortable. Her drinking continued to spiral at times, so the occasional stint in rehab or a mental health facility was not unusual. Sadly, nothing seemed to make much of a difference to her mental state in my eyes, and over the course of time, the sudden mood changes and abuse only compounded. I became hyper-vigilant and able to predict what I perceived as danger. I didn't realize at the time how resilient I was becoming because of my instinct to survive my environment.

At times it seemed that a simple expression was all it took to earn me the repercussions of being locked out of the house, refused meals, chased around the house with a fly swatter, or, let's say, it was not unusual for the infamous leather belt to make its terrifying appearance.

Like a deer in headlights, time stood still. I stiffly watched as the belt flew through the air. I still recall the sound of the leather as it cracked on my bare skin, I held my breath like it wasn't going to hurt as much while he raged, "No one will ever love you" and "You will end up just like me." I observed the welts quickly rise on my body as my skin burned. Gradually they changed color from white to shades of blush pink, dark pink, and purple, just like a gradient on a color wheel. Feelings of unworthiness and disgrace followed, flooding my entire being. Little did I know that these traumatic experiences strengthened my resilience and opened the doorway to the creativity that would become my life's purpose.

Seeking solitude in my bedroom was not so bad, though staring at four small walls seemed like an eternity. With no escaping my environment, I found that tapping into my imagination triggered my creativity and seemed to soothe my inner conflict. I visualized the little sanctuary that felt safe and peaceful, that radiated beauty, and reflected all parts of me. As my eyes slowly scanned the walls, including all the insignificant details of my room, I wondered how the paintings would look on a different wall and then the sideboard, followed by the bed. Would that make the room look larger, or if I cast a shadow on the wall using a lamp, would that make the room feel warmer?

As I imagined new wall paint, I sketched multiple furniture arrangements while using my feet to measure the room's perimeter. So, with great anticipation and an action plan, inch by inch, I dragged one piece of furniture at a time into position until I had implemented my plan. At this point, I discovered I had a creative eye for decorating. The process left me fulfilled and with a feeling of self-achievement, I repeated the rotation every few weeks. As I created my mini room makeovers, I had no idea I was teaching myself the basic principles of interior design.

So naturally, I graduated to other rooms in the house, and it didn't take long until I convinced my friends to let me redecorate their rooms too. Thank God I was becoming more resilient than my mother. As a coping mechanism, I channeled my frustrations into creative endeavors and consciously chose not to become an alcoholic.

I had found some comfort in my newfound talent and the need for creative expression, but observing my mother's mental health issues and alcohol dependence throughout the years was distressing. At times, the torment seemed unbearable, yet there was no denying that the psychological distress continued to affect me. I repeatedly fought deep feelings of unworthiness and loneliness, and I longed to be accepted. In what I perceived as a lack of structure and stability, I didn't feel secure, and my haunting internal beliefs continued to intensify. I was facing an internal battle that seemed impossible to conquer. My inner need to survive psychologically made me more independent, hyper-resilient to life's pressures, and self-reliant.

Growing up, I spent quite a bit with my two grandmothers and was happy that I had developed a closer bond with them over the years. I sought comfort in hearing about their life stories and listened carefully to how they had overcome adversity. Their wisdom gave me the strength and the encouragement I needed. Despite their positive influence, I still continued to suffer many setbacks.

A few months after my twenty-first birthday, a sequence of traumatizing events occurred. Not long after, I developed a sudden onset of severe anxiety when I left the house. I walked to my car, often parked on the street. Suddenly my knees went weak and started to shake, pins and needles gripped my entire body and I felt dizzy. Terrified and consumed with panic, I had no option but to return inside.

Shortly after, a local doctor diagnosed me with panic attacks and an onset of OCD quickly followed. I wondered how on earth I would ever get through this alone. I felt utterly defeated.

Medication was not an option for me as, over many years, I had observed my mother's dependency issues; I was determined to manage my anxiety without any medication, so a guided meditation seemed like a good place to start. It was through meditation that I learned how to tap further into my inner resilience.

I looked at ways to distract my mind and remembered during one of my many decorating frenzies, I had stumbled across a couple of books in the living room bookcase that had sparked my interest. So, with added anticipation, I couldn't wait to rummage through the newly organized bookcase. Books in hand, I retreated to my little sanctuary. I intently started to read the first book, titled *Simple Effective Treatments for Agoraphobia*, written by Dr. Claire Weeks, who was renowned and praised for developing her methods for treating anxiety.

Her writings were informative and easy to read. So, feeling relieved and somewhat optimistic, I couldn't put the book down. I resonated with every word and was now armed with valuable information on anxiety. For the first time, I understood the fight, flight, and freeze response and also gained many helpful tools to assist in management and recovery. I charged through the book in a couple of days. Empowered with knowledge and more confidence, I was determined to jump in my car and go for a short drive. On the way out the front door, I popped the book in my handbag, quickly grabbed a brown paper bag from the kitchen drawer, a bottle of water, and went off.

My first attempt was mildly successful as I managed to drive a few hundred meters before my lips tingled and my vision blurred, so pulling over to the side of the road, I reached for my brown paper bag. I took a few deep breaths, and after some relief, I read a few pages from the book and went off again. At first, I'd pull over every ten minutes and then drive back home. I didn't consider my attempts to be failures, it was a step in the right direction. With sheer determination and tenacity, I managed to drive a bit further every couple of days. With each short drive, I gained more confidence and found that after repeating the cycle for about a month, the fear began to fade. I discovered that by facing challenges, rather than hiding from them, resilience is strengthened.

Feeling empowered, I turned my attention to the second book, *You Can Heal Your Life*, by Louise Hay, in which she writes how your beliefs about yourself can cause emotional problems and manifest as physical illness. It was this book that blew my world apart, with a sense of hopefulness and full of inspiration, I became a keen student. I attended numerous Hay House events with guest speakers such as Dr. Wayne Dyer and Deepak Chopra. The workshops were exciting, motivating, and insightful. Feeling inspired, I continued to invest time and small amounts of money in purchasing self-help and “new age” books, as they were referred to at the time. Over the years I continued to attend Hay House events as they greatly impacted me and were incredibly uplifting. As I reflected on my thoughts, I couldn’t help but notice a shift in my internal beliefs. It was as if I had turned a page in my mindset and, suddenly, I felt even more resilient.

The local bookshop had become my new friend, so while strolling through the isles, my attention was one day drawn to a journal with a beautifully crafted cover perfect for documenting my thoughts and aspirations. I set myself a new task, spent hours cutting images from magazines that spoke to me, and lovingly pasted them into my journal. I wrote poems to express my inner feelings and reflections. It was cathartic and, in many ways, it was a way to manifest my dreams and desires and alchemize my pain into a vision for the future.

I was almost eighteen when I entered the workforce. With no formal qualifications, I somehow managed to talk my way through two interviews and, to my surprise, I secured the position as a PR assistant. I loved my job and over the next two years, I had a couple of promotions and pay rises. Strangely, when things were going quite well in my life, I always anticipated the bubble to burst, which then tested my resilience to cope with the situation.

My mother had been admitted to a mental health and rehab facility as a full-time patient for about three months. There was strictly no visitation allowed during this period, so her daily phone calls to the office took an emotional toll on me. After one very difficult phone call, I was summoned into the managing director's office and told, "You need to work out your private issues, we're letting you go."

I was devastated. Crushed, I felt ashamed and decided not to tell anyone. We must tap into our inner resilience when faced with adversity. It's not always easy, but unexpected challenges can also bring unexpected gifts.

Back to the drawing board and desperate to move out of home and transition into a healthy environment, I set my sights on the fashion industry. I was offered a position in a fashion agency in what felt like a stroke of luck. The staff were friendly and very obliging, I looked up to them and saw them as role models. I was inspired to learn as much as I could, happy to have the opportunity to work directly with clients. Even though I lacked confidence, I knew reaching outside my comfort zone was the only way to gain the skills I needed. So, while misfortune may be tough to face, it can also bring out the best in us and help us grow in ways we never thought possible.

I continued to build on my vision board, keeping me focused and my dream alive while saving money and paving the way toward my independence. I stayed motivated by spending hours looking for affordable apartments to rent while I held on tightly to my dream of having my private sanctuary. I had many hiccups along the way with no previous rental records and my young age all playing against me, I had many knockbacks. With undying persistence, I was ecstatic to receive the news that my application had been successfully approved and I moved into a tiny two-bedroom waterfront apartment.

Throughout the upcoming years, I decided to work a second job not just to save the extra money but also to gain a multitude of experience in different fields and gain new skills. Along the way, employers always seemed to appreciate good people skills and a broad range of admin skills and as a result, found it relatively easy to find extra work. I thrived on being independent and enjoyed my own space.

Over time I became more ambitious, so when I was told the owners were selling the Bondi apartment I lived in, it didn't take long to submit an offer to purchase the small garden apartment. To my surprise, they accepted. I was twenty-six and knew I would have to do a good sales pitch for the local bank manager to secure my first home loan. After a drawn-out and exhausting few weeks of loan applications and a few knockbacks, I finally received approval. Naturally, I couldn't wait to renovate, so I first ran out and bought a can of paint. As a result of my tenacious and reliant nature, it paid off!

Feeling settled and in the safety of my apartment, I looked for positions that could earn me more money. My love for magazines and photography led me to apply for a position in a prominent magazine company. I had little experience that was relevant for this particular role, but I was determined not to let this opportunity slip through my fingers. I felt this was my dream job, so after my second interview had gone by and still no word came, I found myself requesting another interview where I found myself promising to work additional hours to learn the software.

With an editorial department of around fifty-five people, which included very colorful characters and challenging personalities, I had no option but to put on a brave front. I still lacked some confidence, and old thoughts of unworthiness continued to resurface. The pressure was on, and no time to waste with set print deadlines that would have been challenging at the best of times, and I had managed to back myself into a corner. I had come this far, so there was no way I was giving in. I continued to push my boundaries, which extended way out of my comfort zone. As a result, over the next four years, I grew in ways I had never thought possible. It was my mother who had taught me to fight for what I wanted and become incredibly resilient, unbeknownst to her.

At this time, a handsome stranger from the art department appeared in front of my desk one day. After one after-work drink at the local pub, I instinctively knew we would get married. Which is exactly what we did, eighteen months later.

In keeping with challenging my abilities and having worked closely with the marketing staff over the years, I decided I would be a good fit. My working life demonstrated that anything was possible with sheer enthusiasm and motivation. I always had the attitude of "what's the worst that can happen" and took the chance. Feeling ambitious and with a sense of nothing to lose, I decided to approach the marketing director and ask for a job.

After a quick chat and as expected, with no formal marketing qualifications, he apologized and thanked me for taking the initiative. Not giving in that easily, I requested a quick, second meeting the next day. I confidently suggested he set me up a small project and if I passed, he could offer me a junior role. He agreed, so within the week, I nervously marched back into his office and presented my ideas. I was pretty chuffed when he offered me a new position as promotions manager. In general, I learned that people respond well to motivation, and my motivation made me more ambitious and resilient when faced with challenges.

While working in marketing, I was able to organize and style photoshoots, and with my natural ability for styling, I decided to study interior decorating. During a sick day and one of my daytime TV marathons, I watched an episode of Oprah where the discussion was about "What's your passion?" I found this episode so inspiring that it motivated me to start my own decorating business. Once again, it was time to put my resilience to the test!

Aware of the time involved in getting a new business off the ground, I worked part-time for a well-known PR company; this gave me some income while I set out to build my own styling business. I presented myself as a freelancer styling homeware shoots and property styling. My business took off fairly quickly and grew as word spread and the referrals poured in. I made good use of my media background and contacts and was invited to write various articles on tips for styling and decorating, published in homeware magazines.

I had been married for about six years and life seemed fairly perfect. With a reasonably successful business, I often had to pinch myself, though I still had old belief patterns lurking in the shadows, anticipating my world would collapse at any moment. I've sometimes found the pressure of running and building a small business difficult. Staying focused and being disciplined were exhausting sometimes. I've also discovered that not having the same support networks as a large company was sometimes a real challenge.

My husband's career was accelerating simultaneously, and we both became very work-oriented, working incredibly long hours and confronting many internal challenges. We decided to attend marriage counseling which we both found very helpful. However, this triggered some old wounds in us. After attending regular sessions, I was diagnosed with childhood PTSD. This opened up a new can of worms and fast-forwarded my journey into self-discovery. I had previously deemed my childhood a curse and in many ways, felt I was given some kind of a prison sentence that I could not escape. After all these years and accomplishing so much, my past was rearing its ugly head in my marriage.

Our psychologist was brilliant, so I decided to attend counseling independently. I knew I was opening Pandora's Box and jumped all in with great courage. I wanted to connect the dots and better understand PTSD and my triggers. Once again, I was faced with the old belief patterns that I had tried so hard to run away from and so, working through the process, I re-lived a lot of past traumas. With flashbacks and old memories continuing to surface, I realized how much I had buried deep in my subconsciousness. Cognitive behavioral therapy was hard at times but well worth it. I finally had an insight into how I was wired and why. It all made perfect sense to me and with it came some relief. This didn't make the process any easier.

My interior design business and creative expressions were my passion and I learned how to use old trauma wounds to tap into my imagination, transform rooms, and create amazing spaces just as I had done as a child. For the first time, I could see how I had alchemized trauma and turned it into creative power. Perhaps in some twisted way, this was another blessing in disguise.

My business continued to grow as word spread. As a result, I was very confident in my ability, yet I've found many work situations extremely confronting. It was common for married clients to argue during meetings, or for the occasional builder to believe his design ideas were better than yours. I had learned many new communication skills and was armed with tools I could use with a client or a tradesman during times of difficulty. Through my resilience, I've developed the ability to be patient and understanding toward others. I learned to communicate my thoughts and ideas calmly and with composure, which helped me navigate these challenging situations.

I was proud of the growth I've made through attending marriage counseling on and off throughout the years. I consciously attended the odd counseling session when I hit a severe roadblock or sought additional support. I was aware that PTSD had to be managed and was only too keen to learn other skills that I needed. We also continued with marriage counseling when we hit a road bump, or when our communication stagnated.

Committed to my healing journey, I continued to meditate, read many books, and listen to podcasts. I've gained much knowledge over the years and enrolled in an advanced counseling course; a skill I thought would be invaluable.

My husband's work intensified, and we became like two ships at night. The long working hours and lack of balance eventually took their toll on me. I had built many walls to protect myself over many years and found it only created more anxiety at times and provided only short-term coping mechanisms. I struggled to connect and started reflecting more on my spiritual path. Faced with some serious autoimmune issues, I ultimately slowed my business down, spending countless hours and money visiting doctors and specialists. After some time, I became increasingly anxious, and the panic attacks returned quickly. With my health and marriage taking a downward spiral, I was at an all-time low.

Throughout the many years of inner conflict, I've faced many challenges and adversities, I had found strength in wisdom and knew how resilient I had become, even if I wasn't feeling it. I had survived extreme circumstances and was responsible for my own life. By tapping into pain, I could release old belief systems. I had given my power away and knew I had to take back control over my life. I picked myself up and sprung back into action. I had no option but to educate myself in holistic health. I listened to countless podcasts, leading me to book an appointment with an integrated doctor specializing in functional medicine. I upped my meditation, ate healthily, and walked to clear and manage my wandering thoughts and anxiety. I consciously decided to create inner peace and shift my focus and my health slowly improved.

Sadly, after twenty-two years and the lockdowns during the pandemic, my marriage came to an end. Throughout this time, life has slowed down so much that I now have the space to question everything. I had to temporarily lose myself to find myself again. I rediscovered the true meaning of self-worth and the value of speaking your truth.

Life takes unexpected turns, and you can suddenly find yourself on a new path. Throughout my journey, I learned not to resist change, as change is only energy. Changing my perception was one of the most powerful skills I had discovered and perhaps the hardest. For every loss, looking at the new with open eyes and an open heart and embracing change can be incredibly empowering. Magic can happen if we welcome new beginnings. Resilience means asking for help and reaching out for support when you need it. Release what doesn't serve you, that's the key.

Our ability to build resilience to disappointments and failures can be enhanced by giving and having gratitude. Having the wisdom and courage to turn your pain into power can open up new pathways you have never dreamed possible.

Learning, relearning, and then relearning some more, is the most important lesson I have embraced on my journey.

**“Strong people are not born.
They are forged by dark days and
polished by resilience.”**

~ KMC

CHAPTER SIX

Behind The Smile

This is my story.

By Ominda Soemijadi

Resilience is how we process trauma and is the outcome of adapting our minds after difficult, challenging, and traumatic experiences. It's a life skill that has helped me both personally and professionally. Sometimes, if we take on too much too soon, we set ourselves up to fail. It is a skill we learn, and we need more practice to improve and maintain our sense of perspective. We need to challenge any negative thoughts to find solutions. I would like to explore my story with you, which is leading me to create greater mental and emotional resilience for myself.

Let's start from the beginning. I feel that it all stems from the beginning, which molds us into the person we are and affects the choices we make. When creating resilience, we face our challenges, we face setbacks, we need to adapt, and resilience is recovering from setbacks we face. The question is, how far back should we go? I will go back to my first memory. Isn't it strange that our first memories often seem to involve pain? Well, for me, this was the case. I learned the technique of flight or fight from early on and was conditioned to carry this throughout my life.

Some of my stories may shock you. I am not here to make others fear life; however, I hope my story helps someone develop more resilience in their life, even just one person, to recognize they are not alone. I do not want sympathy; I want us to acknowledge that many of us have sad stories behind our smiles.

My first memory:
I felt awkward…
I felt loved…
I was made to feel guilty…
I was made to feel scared…
My childhood was taken…
I was made to feel it was my fault…

I froze and closed my eyes so I could leave my body and imagine I was elsewhere; I would be that child running and playing in a field full of beautiful blue and green dragonflies. If I could leave my body, I could go to my happy place, which numbed the pain. I conditioned myself to numb myself from physical and mental pain early on, which would stay with me until today. I learned through my childhood trauma of sexual abuse to keep fighting in the face of adversity.

As I grew up into an adult beyond my years, I grew wiser and learned survival and resilience. This skill would get me through the disappointments and pains of life. I conditioned myself not to feel vulnerable even though I was being abused. Then, one day, a miracle happened. I was once a religious girl, and I prayed that God would save me. Well, there was a moment when I felt he did, as I woke to find my father and mother were moving us away. Moving has become a regular thing in my life to this very day. But it is still a mystery to me as to why we did this so often. Were my parents running, too?

I would be mentally and physically abused numerous times again throughout my life, almost as though I had a target on my back. At the time, did I blame anyone else? No, I didn't, not even the people meant to protect me. They abandoned me, so this is when, from a young age, I learned to trust no one but myself. Ultimately, the only person that could be there for me was ME...

For a long time, I was a sad soul. I learned to hide behind a pretty smile, condition myself, and convince myself I was a happy child. I learned from a young age that the male species could not be trusted. My father let me down. He didn't protect me, and this experience of attachment and abandonment would follow me through life. I learned in adulthood that I needed help to recondition my thought process to avoid repeating negative history. I came to realize it was like being an addict in rehabilitation. Whenever I was in a toxic situation with a man or woman, I needed to reboot. If I didn't forgive and trust again, how could I ever have a successful relationship in the future? I was creating resilience by taking a positive perspective on relationships and viewing each challenging relationship as a learning opportunity to improve my future.

I moved to a small country town, bringing happiness, safety, and security to my life. In this town, people wanted out. They wanted to move to the city. They had what I was yearning for: the simple life, which was boring for some people. My first day of school in this town was eventful. On the first day, there was a brown snake in my classroom. I didn't feel scared; it felt like a symbol. I was free for the first time. How could I be scared like the other children? It was a beautiful creature that, for me, symbolized resilience.

And for a while, my life was happy and safe, and life was simple. I loved it. For a time, we lived with safe family members who did not attempt to hurt me. Then we got the call that we would be placed into social housing as we did not have much money. Our new home was beautiful. It was home, however, as time passed, I realized being in a small town brought problems. Some people were narrow-minded; I looked different; my skin color was different. I would quickly learn how people experience fear differently.

I became a target of racist and sexualized abuse, but I had conditioned myself before, so I told no one of the torments I had gone through and would bottle it all inside, hiding it behind my smile. I let it happen. I let the thugs bully me daily and convinced myself that it was what I deserved. Some days I considered whether life was not worth living, but a strength within me told me to keep going and that maybe I deserve happiness. There was a battle within me.

I would leave home and go to school unconfident and fearful; I would be spat on daily and have my school skirt pulled up for everyone to see my underwear. I was humiliated. I often thought, where did these teenagers learn to be such cowards? Where did they understand this behavior, and how was this behavior acceptable? I dealt with this torment daily, crying in silence alone like always. I soon learned greater resilience by becoming friends with my bullies, working my way into the group by targeting the most emotionally vulnerable bully; I guess my fight-or-flight mode kicked in that day. I recreated my persona to become a social, popular girl and singer. I was a very talented person. Others wanted to be my friend or be me. When I grew up, I became a very pretty young lady, so I decided to use my looks and become the popular girl at school and this became a regular survival skill for most of my adult life.

I would, in silence, help other teenage girls being bullied. I would try to be their protector, a trait I was always familiar with. Living on a council estate is very different, and I feel that if you have never lived on one, you would never truly know what it's like, unless you were one of us. My experience was freedom but at a cost. We had to grow up way too fast on the estate. Sometimes we are conditioned to be a certain way because we do not know any other way, forced to parent ourselves. Creating resilience was key to survival. My experiences have taught me life lessons to survive and, at times, to not judge a book by its cover because, along my journey, I also met a lot of individuals that touched my soul. In the 80s and 90s, things were different in Australia. Their housing estates were beautiful with beautiful new homes; however, it was hard to predict what life would be like behind every front door, each house full of their own stories.

Many of the children I encountered in the estate had created resilience without knowing how to start surviving in life's journey. We all had to learn the tools in some way to effectively cope with the mental stresses and challenges thrust upon us.

We all, children, teenagers, and often adults, would congregate in the big park in the middle, which I could see from my bedroom window. This park in itself had a lot of stories, especially in the pitch black of the night. There were boys and girls smoking marijuana and other drugs consumed, and I would often see people, often kids, being intimate, being way too young to be doing what they were doing. There were fights, gangs, and other teenagers like me just trying to hang onto the last of their youth. I remember clearly that I have never seen any parents in that park. Maybe they were in the houses. I'm not sure I just never saw them.

Being a council estate teenager, there were always hurdles to climb, like bullying, which I found unbearable, but I survived and found a way. I made a friend with a neighbor. She was an awkward girl. I felt sorry for her and her brother. They became my friends. They were both autistic, but they and their family were beautiful people. Her brother had a crush on me. His gaze would make me uncomfortable, but he was harmless, almost childlike. I remember that they had so many pets, one of which was a praying mantis. I would grow to love this insect. It is, to this day, a creature of such beauty to me. How it could camouflage itself when in danger is how I sometimes feel.

One day, my parents told me we were moving again, but this time it was different. My parents bought a little house. It was more like a tin shack, but it would be our home. It would be all ours.

Our new home was a small place, but it was where I finally felt at home, and this place called Melrose Place was my safety. I shared a bed with my two sisters. I grew up and became a woman living there with a rollercoaster of emotional ups and downs. I met my first best friend, my German Shepherd puppy, and also some very loving young people who, to this day, are still in my life.

Never mistake the sharing of my negative thoughts as me being negative; however, writing how you feel helps you process things, and it enables you to try and put your past in the past. I will tell you the crime against me was wrong; however, what is done is done, and I had to survive and place in my mind things that sometimes happen to mold you into who you become. I am me because of what happened to me. My resilience muscle has grown and minor problems that used to bother me no longer do.

The man to whom I told my secret proved to be a key person in a significant shift in my life. At the same time, it felt like one of my lowest times. This young man asked me to tell my parents. I refused, so he threatened me. He advised that if I did not reveal my secret to my family, he would have no choice but to tell my secret himself. I am not sure what his original intentions with me were, but I cannot deny he helped me let out this horrible secret that was building up and festering inside me. He advised me to release this secret; otherwise, it would destroy me.

The thought of approaching my father made me so nervous, so scared he was a weak man, and I questioned if he would still love his little girl. The truth did end up coming out, and my father disappointed me. This would be the first of many disappointments by him. I will not detail what happened between my father and I, but he proved to be weak and cowardly. He made a terrible decision to make me confront my abuser to prove to him I was telling the truth. I will never be able to forgive this betrayal. Coming out about my abuse was the beginning of my parent's relationship breaking down, and for years I blamed myself for this. My father did not understand resilience, and he did not understand me. I had built the ability to bend but not break, and I could bounce back when needed.

We then moved on with our lives like nothing had ever happened, like there was no past to discuss. I was forced to bury my feelings and live a normal life again, even though I didn't know what normal was. All I knew was survival. I write this as I sit in my favorite coffee shop, watching the world go by me. I love viewing people's habits. I try to imagine what everyone's stories are. I know there are others like me out there, and that I'm not the only one suffering silently; I have met them. These people are all around us. They are stay-at-home mums, sitting in libraries, a doctor, maybe sitting next to me in this café, your neighbors, and perhaps even your family. I know others have created resilience like me by managing strong emotions and impulses.

The place where I have my coffee has a saying, "Never a dull cup," I feel that's a bit like life, and to be honest, do we want it to be any other way? I was the eldest child in my family. So I knew what was happening and protected my younger sisters as much as possible.

Life can change in a heartbeat…

I continued my life holding a secret that made me feel so suffocated, while on the outside I portrayed something that was far from what I was actually feeling. I guess it helped me get through things and to survive. For years, I would be in a serious relationship, not always with the right person. My abuser did this to me. From such a young age, I was conditioned to believe people's actions against women should be treated as meaningless; in therapy, I learned I should not see myself this way. It took me a long time to recondition myself, and I continue to do this today. Every man, every example I had growing up, disappointed me, and abandoned me in some form, and no matter how positive I was to myself for a long time, I felt I was not worthy. I thought I was damaged goods.

As I sit here, a grown woman, I am finally finding myself, which is liberating. I have started to encourage myself to do what I want:

to expose this secret that I hold and have everyone responsible take ownership of making me keep this horrible secret for so long. Finally, I felt free, and I do not feel scared anymore. I will do this for me, my children, and every victim who can never speak out against what happened. I am not worried. I am not ashamed, as I have done absolutely nothing wrong. I have learned throughout my life not to look for our happiness in others; we have to find that happiness within ourselves before we can truly be happy.

I have learned, through creating resilience, how to move on in my life and stay focused on today and my future. Focusing on events in my life which I control has been a good way of practicing resilient behaviors.

It may seem like I skip back and forth through my life in this book, but I feel this is relevant in telling my story and showing how I have created resilience in my life. Many in my family, like myself, experienced trauma growing up, which can change you. I suffer from long-term Post-Traumatic Stress Disorder, and I describe my condition as having a scar that can open, sometimes requiring a plaster to close it up again. As a result, you feel like you think differently to others around you. I can be more skeptical, less trusting, and more streetwise. This can be an unhealthy way to look at things but can also be a positive trait sometimes.

Some people who are were sexually abused and mentally traumatized tend to “fake it till they make it.” Some commit to self-harm to numb their mental pain, some look for love in everyone to fill their emptiness, and some may lose sleep at night with anxiety. They will try to avoid every possible loving partner that crosses their path for fear of being hurt. I created resilience through my trauma, bouncing back from the physical abuse that has led me to bounce back from negative emotional experiences.

Unfortunately, life is more complicated than ever. Life is proving to be challenging with social media issues, mental health complications, and growing crime rates. I have children now, and trying to control my anxiety about their safety is complex, and I am aware I must continue to communicate and be mindful of their environments. I never felt I had someone to turn to, and I think my parents failed me. So, I decided to come forward with my story and involve the legal system, which is scary and, at the same time, liberating. I may not win my case, but I will achieve closure and, hopefully, justice. It takes a lot of courage, but it also builds resilience and self-belief to confront our trauma.

Friends have often asked why now? And these questions I would like to share with you.

Friend: “I’m curious what inspired you to take action.”
Me: “I believe everyone that knew what happened to me should have done something when I was a child. Every one of them should be held accountable, as well as my abuser. I needed closure, and I had exhausted the counseling route. I have two children. I needed to do it for them, and every woman who was too scared to come forward. This is the first time I think of what’s best for me, putting my needs first and not what I feel everyone expects or wants me to do. I also feel this time is mine, and I am strong enough, and not living in shame anymore.”

Friend: “What is your desired outcome?”
Me: “Closure! I hope to get closure and for all the adults in my life to realize they did wrong by keeping the nightmare I endured a secret.”

This is my story of how I have created resilience in my life. All of us will find our own ways. This is my journey. Years passed, and the fight exhausted me, but I remained strong and hung on. This time in my life has been a real test. Some days I wake up wondering if I’m strong enough, but I know I am. Even on my weakest days, I can do it. I have survived this long. I have found some beautiful people that stand by my side, so when I doubt myself, they help remind me why I am doing this - FREEDOM! When we are resilient, we can create freedom. Authorities warned me it would take a long time, and I had to try and remain patient. Sometimes I feel people don't believe me, but I know this is my anxiety talking.

I have chosen complete disclosure because this is a historic case, and it's the only chance I have to get the justice I deserve against this poor excuse of a human being. When I first came out about my secret, it was hard. I felt like that little girl again, vulnerable and alone. I had to relive my experience. This was tough, but I am so proud of myself for being strong enough to do so. But at the end of the day, I am not that little girl anymore. I am an independent, strong woman, a mother, and I must remind myself of this.

In my case, the crime would be accepted, and this alone, I knew, was a victory in itself. I have learned through research that historical crimes can be thrown out at the first hurdle. I then felt relief alongside a feeling of fear. I knew this journey ahead of me would be hard, and I needed to focus on the good in my life; I must do this for me and my children.

There are times I feel emotionally overwhelmed and triggered, as I would hear nothing about how the case was progressing for months on end unless I made an effort to chase down the information myself. This wait has brought challenges and flashbacks. I found this long wait for news unbearable. Some days, I wake up thinking I am doing the right thing and justice will prevail. Then other days, I wake up and feel nobody cares and I am the only one fighting for justice. I wake up knowing my abuser probably lives a life like everyone else, and in this life, the happiness he may live, is not what he is deserving of.

"Carpe Diem."

Whether I win or lose, I tried hard to get justice. I will continue to smile no matter my pain and must motivate myself to keep fighting. I need to lift myself to fight for every person who has lost their childhood and take small steps and hope these steps of fighting for justice do not take my whole lifetime. I must keep using the tools I taught myself and learned from others. I created resilience in my life to get me through the challenges I have experienced and for further challenges I may have to endure to remind me how strong I truly am.

I waited months to hear from the detectives assigned to my case. I knew this journey would be hard, since we had to combine two countries and file evidence. Hence, people understand the crime is real, and the difficulties that come from coming forward with a violent sexual offense against a minor, and knowing the pedophile is out there roaming free is difficult to deal with. Nevertheless, a crime happened, and I will not stop until justice has prevailed.

It's not the outcome…
It's not revenge…
It's not even the story…
It's the closure…
It is not easy…
It will never be easy whether you choose to hold it in your heart or share your experience…
You must do what is right for you…
Never give up on yourself…
And creating resilience is a key substance in getting through the challenges…
If you want the rainbow, you must endure the rain and hail...

Later, the dreams would come again to haunt me. These nightmares come and go, causing me to find sleep difficult. Resilience is hard to achieve when you are asleep, as my brain cannot use the tools I have learned. I was diagnosed with long-term PTSD. And I am unsure how it made me feel, especially with the word "long-term." The wait for therapy to help me with my PTSD would take several months, and I was in a new relationship and feared destroying it with my emotional baggage. I worried whether he would be strong enough to get through this trauma and remain loyal to me.

Creating resilience can benefit you when you suffer from PTSD by seeking support from others you trust, finding support groups, and attending counseling if it works for you. In addition, learning to create resilience can normally enhance the healing process of our trauma.

The police made some significant mistakes in this case, mistakes I had assumed might happen due to this case remaining open. I am unable to delve too much into this case due to legal reasons so this will be a story for another day. However, I can confirm that they didn't listen to the victim. I knew my attacker. I knew how he would react if suspected of anything. Sometimes it's hard to trust when you have been let down so many times. I find it hard to trust the new detective allocated to my case after the recent mistakes made, especially after a year and a half of me chasing down progress reports and answers. My sleep is affected, and as time goes on, I get angry that a sex offender is roaming the streets our children play in.

My parents were interviewed. My mother, I knew, would say what she needed to show support, but like she has for my entire life, just like my father, they will think of themselves first and their feelings, never putting me first. I understand my parents have their demons they are dealing with, but it's now my time to put myself first.

My mother…
A woman lost…
A woman tainted…
A woman hurt…
A woman weak…
A woman in regret…
A woman I once loved…

A woman damaged…
A woman hated…
A woman that doesn't know different…
A woman I forgave…
A woman I now understand…
A relationship lost

...

A woman that is now too far…
My father…
A man lost...
A man hurt…
A man who is weak…
A man in regret…
A man who is really a boy…
A man I once loved…
A man damaged…
A man hated…
A man pitied…
A man who is a product of his environment…
A man I forgave…
A man I will never understand…
A relationship lost…
A man that is now too far…

I was not the only victim in this story. My whole family were victims trying to use their resilience tools to survive the individual traumas they had experienced, creating a resilience that works for them alone. But, of course, an individual's resilience is different. Some make their resilience by their past experiences, some by what they are taught by others, and some by their environment and situations.

So mid-case, I received a message on behalf of both my parents that made me realize my parents would never understand why I had to do what I was doing. It was clear that their thinking was for the sake of my father, and how he was influenced by the culture he was brought up in.“

“A woman must know her place, she must understand things just happen when you’re a woman.”

And for this reason I had to cut him out of my life. He seemed to feel sorrow and regret, but he was conditioned to believe what happened to me just happens and I should accept it. Referring to my mother, she was weak; my father was a nice man to her; however she too was conditioned from a young age to the fact that life throws these horrible things at some people and they need to accept it. I could never see eye to eye with the people who brought me into this world. It was stated that I would have to get over things that happened in the past and that my parents were old now, so I should drop it. It dawned on me that this situation would never change the way they thought. All my life would never change; however, I am no longer willing to put my feelings in a box. I would forgive them, but I would have to live a separate life from my parents for my well-being.

The resilience in the life I had created that worked for me helped me through the struggles I felt from how my parents made me feel and how the authorities made me feel. I have to fight through my feelings of feeling unimportant and meaningless, or when triggers pop up from people stating they are too busy to deal with my case. It has been made evident to me that many victims do not come forward to be made to feel like this after all the struggles we go through to get the courage to come forward. No one could ever truly understand unless you were in my position. Creating resilience from the knockbacks and rejections can be done, and ignorance can be fought by simply showing up, continuing to show up, and never giving up. All of this has helped me through the turmoil I was facing.

I have recently discovered my wait may take many years, which is upsetting, but I am learning to accept what I cannot change. I have done beyond what I thought I could have ever imagined by getting my day in court, and I hope I get the justice I need to be served.

As said by Dr. Steve Maraboli, “Life doesn’t get easier or more forgiving; we get stronger and more resilient.”

**"Resilience is a muscle,
flex it enough and it will take less
effort to get over emotional
punches each time."**

- Alecia Moore

CHAPTER SEVEN

Lead By Example

by Jon Ch. Henningsen

Life is unpredictable and full of challenges that must be dealt with and handled no matter how unpleasant it feels.

No matter how we plan, and live our lives, unexpected circumstances that are beyond our control will be part of life (are we well-equipped to handle these?)

In this chapter I will share with you how resilience and developing a resilient mindset (I had a light version, but nothing compared to the advanced pro-version I´m equipped with today) came to play a transformative role in my life.

It´s my personal story of how developing a resilient mindset helped me face and overcome challenges and crisis.

I will share with you - what I have experienced, what I have learned, what methods and strategies I use today, and what you can do to develop a more resilient mindset because unforeseen challenges will find us all during our lifetime.

In April of 2013 I was diagnosed with cancer.

That was my introduction to some serious personal development and me getting ready to participate in the "Final Fight".

This confrontation was needed to let go of my collection of failures and the shame and guilt that was trapped inside me (replacing it with realistic and useful self-judgement/criticism).

Looking back from the perspective/knowledge I now have - it (illness) had been many years on its way.

Over the years I've learned that after breakdowns (obstacles/ challenges), very often breakthroughs emerge (won't always be appreciated and, on the radar, right away) as a result (personal development/increased resilience).

Hardships, and overcoming them, makes it possible to level up your resilient mindset (stored wisdom/accessible on demand) and level up in life.

My chapter is sub-divided into four mini-chapters.

Are you ready?

Let's dive in!

Mini-Chapter One: The Diagnosis

At the beginning of 2013, I felt a bit off with some weird symptoms that I had never experienced before – after my bloodwork had been analyzed we found out I had some inflammatory markers that were high.

My doctor prescribed some anti-inflammatory medication, but a few weeks later the treatment had not solved the issue.

He called some experts at a bigger hospital with more sophisticated medical equipment. We then drove to the hospital for my appointment there. After several hours and several test/ scans/ultrasound/bloodwork we were called into the chief oncologist's office.

He told a younger, inexperienced oncologist to close the door.

He then asked, "Is it ok if he stays here with us – he has not tried this before?"

"Sure," I said.

They sat down across from me; I could tell by the look on his face that something was not right, and then he said, "Based on the medical examination and the tests I'm 99 % sure you have a tumor in your left testicle that needs to be surgically removed – you'll be scheduled for an operation tomorrow."

"What just happened!"

It´s difficult to precisely describe my emotional state when I received the news that would change my life from that moment on.

My heart sank, and I felt like the air had been knocked out of me.

It was like I had watched a movie played in super slow-motion.

"Cancer, cancer, cancer…"

I was only 34, and I never thought cancer was something that could happen to me.

The day of diagnosis at the hospital, I (we, my then fiancé and now wife was with me) was in shock, despair, helplessness, and a huge, black cloud of uncertainty entered my life.

A long list of words ran through my head in seconds:

Elisabeth (our 3-year young daughter), cancer, survival, fertility, treatment, masculinity, testosterone, metastasis, what is this opponent I'm facing?

It was my first operation which also made me a bit anxious (luckily my father, the calmest man I know, drove me to the hospital that morning which help calm my nerves).

I felt fragile and vulnerable, I was overwhelmed with fear and uncertainty - it was like I had lost control over my life in an instant.

I feared what the future held and how I would cope with the diagnosis.

Suddenly, a long life with decades to come was not a guarantee (it never is, but at the time I never thought much about it).

After waiting nine days we were told it was caught early – the operation was successful, the tumor was removed and now five years of tests, examinations, and active surveillance (new treatment option at the time for early-stage testicular cancer). A biopsy showed no signs of cancer in the remaining testicle.

I was diagnosed with a non-seminoma(teratoma) and told that long-term survival was 95 % (recurrence usually happens fast/after a few months), so my very first goal was to focus on the 95 % that make it and not the 5 % that don't (there are no guarantees, but I was determined to do my absolute best).

After this uplifting news (no metastasis) I experienced my first mindset shift - from comfort/complacency to investing all my available resources (I/we had not many resources at the time) into survival and keeping hope alive. The development of my resilient mindset began. The experience helped me develop a flexible mindset as I navigated this obstacle.

Being told that there were no signs of metastasis (and I would need no chemotherapy) re-charged my mental energy.

I stored that energy for later activities and after almost six weeks of wound healing, I began moving again – what a wonderful feeling!

The message of "only" localized cancer instantly put extra motivation in my resource pool – a factor that helped me to change my lifestyle (although I was a personal trainer at the time – I did not eat well myself, especially during the weekends), so there was much progress to be made. My resilience to complete difficult tasks and operate outside of my comfort zone was also weak.

You can let hardship define you, you can let it grow you, and you can let it teach you and then move on in life. Development of resilience is a very useful skill in life. At the time of diagnosis, all my internal resilience came from doing what I at the time considered "hard" exercise. That was until I began exploring "The Great Unknown Zone" (a mental concept I have developed and that I use in my coaching). It's scary to enter but the rewards (a backpack full of lifelong resilience/post traumatic growth spurt) are without comparison.

What sets some people apart is their ability to bounce back from setbacks and overcome challenges quicker and more effortlessly than others. This quality is known as resilience.

Resilience is also the ability to adapt to change, overcome obstacles, and recover from adversity. It is the capacity to thrive in the face of adversity, uncertainty, and stress.

Resilient people generally have a positive outlook on life (I did not have that back in 2013/a business project hadn't gone as planned five years earlier and that failed project haunted me for years/ economically and emotionally). Resilient people can manage their emotions (I had not learned to manage my emotions at the time) and have the ability to bounce back from setbacks (I somewhat managed to do this from time to time, although superficially – I only managed to surf the small waves).

Studies have shown that characteristics of resilience, particularly social connections, and a strong sense of self-worth, help people confront chronic illness. A review of research on resilience and chronic disease suggested that a person's resilience can influence both the progression and outcome of illnesses.

Research published in April 2019 in the journal *Frontiers in Psychiatry* linked resilience, notably personal strengths, and social factors, to improved psychological and treatment-related outcomes for cancer patients.

That was my foundation at the time.

Without that foundation, although fragile, to stand on, I wouldn't have been able to face the diagnosis with the same amount of hope, focus and energy. I had a lot to live for as our daughter was just 3-years-young at the time. Being a father and role model is not something I take lightly (no one should – the world needs more responsible and pro-active adults).

I also experimented with different diets, fasting protocols, supplementation, and training regiments (optimizing sleep was something I focused on later in my journey/the science of sleep as it relates to health and prevention has exploded since I was diagnosed just over ten years ago).

Experimentation is also an effective tool to become more resilient because you´re challenging your comfort zone (that is why it is so challenging to change your habits – its more comfortable to keep doing what you're doing - it requires no effort/it´s automatic).

Especially the more extreme fasting protocols in year one and two post-diagnosis have taught me a new kind of resilience.

Until the diagnosis, I was eating 5-6 meals throughout the day to keep my blood sugar stable, and I thought I would have no energy if I fasted (I even thought it was dangerous to fast/avoid meals – through this process I discovered another level of resilience).

Later, I found out that my ups and downs in energy were because of my eating habits (I was diagnosed with pre-diabetes as a 10-year-old boy, so I had lived like this for decades/medical advice in the late 1980´s) and because I was not fat adapted – I was running primarily on carbs and sugar – once I became fat adapted, I began burning fat as fuel.

That is how I have lost much of the weight (20.6 kg), unfortunately I have also lost much fat free mass and strength which I could have avoided with the knowledge I have now/it took me years to re-gain (luckily, it´s possible).

Changing my lifestyle and habits ended up "curing" my pre-diabetes (I had the condition for 24 years), and know I help people do the same by passing on my knowledge and wisdom (lifestyle medicine principles).

At one point I had become so fat adapted that I could train at high intensity (I mean completely all-out to my ability) for 10 to 30 minutes, after minimum 20 hours of fasting.

My personal best after 20 hours of fasting is 9.9 km in 10 minutes/27.9 km in 30 minutes on a spin bike (it was a purely will based effort and the will to live/it was even before I began using different kinds of herbal teas at strategic times during the day to maximize performance).

Later, I have found out that such extreme fasting protocols + hours of exercise (at the time I still did a lot of cardio) did not help me maintain and build muscle mass so I began experimenting with time-restricted feeding (TRF) instead, which helped me tremendously.

I still practice TRF as I´ve found it works well for me (I´ve done this for a decade at this point).

What is exercise?

A very good resilience development tool – it's you against the time/the speed/the weight/your opponent – it just works (think of how the military used to educate and train personnel).

In the next mini-chapters I will unpack the most important lessons that I have learned, and what you can focus on if you are ready to explore and learn how to create a more resilient mindset.

Mini-Chapter Two: The Journey Begins

After the initial shock had worn off, I thought about what I could do to overcome this challenge. I began researching treatments (what could I do myself to lower the risk of recurrence and improve my health?) and talking to other cancer survivors. I also focused on my mental and emotional well-being by practicing what is now called eco-therapy (I didn´t use meditation) and active mindfulness (using music to tune in and release/mental cleansing).

Music was a huge part of my recovery process (I've always used music to achieve mental order and to enhance my performance when training/today, I can also do it without music – THAT´S RESILIENCE).

I listen to heavy metal and melodic death metal (it's a rare art form). Life is too short to spend precious time listening to what is popular on the radio these days. A very special thanks to Iron Maiden (I've been to many of their concerts in Denmark over the last 20 years) for enriching my life with a legendary and ultra-rare combination of music and lyrics.

As I went through treatment, I realized I was stronger than I had thought. I could handle the physical and emotional challenges of cancer with resilience and determination. I also began appreciating the small moments in life and the people who were there to support me. I realized the importance of taking care of myself emotionally, which helped me stay grounded and to focus on the present moment. This allowed me to accept my diagnosis and move forward with a more resilient mindset.

I began showing up with a newfound joy in many of the activities I had taken for granted before the diagnosis.

Spending time with my family, having a conversation (truly present), going for a walk in the forest, in nature, in our garden, or simply taking a few moments to be still and reflect. This helped me to stay positive and to have a more balanced outlook on life.

Overall, my cancer diagnosis helped me to open up emotionally (I call it emotional constipation if people I coach have not learned to open up emotionally) and to transform my fragile mindset into a more resilient one. It taught me the importance of self-care and of appreciating life with newfound respect. It also showed me I could recruit much more energy from within when needed (it's in there, which calms me down).

Mini-Chapter Three: Growth and Strength

As I progressed through my cancer journey, I observed how it had transformed me in unexpected ways. I became more confident and self-assured, knowing that I could face most challenges that came my way (increased focus on personal responsibility/taking action instead of having a victim mentality). I´m calmer in high-pressure situations and much more dangerous, although I´m much smaller (I´m 6'4) as I have lost more than 20 kgs since I've changed to a healthier lifestyle (risk reduction) post-diagnosis. By facing the challenge head-on, the experience equipped me with the mental and emotional tools necessary to remain resilient and focused and perform at my best, even under significant pressure.

How come I´m more dangerous (if needed)?

Today I know (I´m aware) how much I have to lose – nothing more than my best is good enough when it comes to family, community, and country. I have become more compassionate and empathetic towards others who were going through difficult times, and I've stopped judging people in advance (now I tell myself you don't know their story and what situation they are in).

I have also begun taking risks (less and less afraid of mistakes/ recovering perfectionist) and began pursuing my passions with more energy and focus, knowing that life is too short to waste on things that don't matter (I even began writing poems again and dusted off my old coin collection). I became more grateful for the people and experiences in my life, and I learned to live in the present moment.

Resilience is the ability to adapt to and bounce back from adversity, trauma, stress, or any other difficult situation. It is the capacity to cope with challenges and maintain a positive outlook in the face of adversity. Resilience is not a trait that people are born with; it is something that can be developed and cultivated.

I was given a second chance in life, to focus on being the best I can be (that will be channeled to others around me) and developing my personal goals. I make sure I spend more time nurturing relationships with family and friends, and focus on working hard to reach my goals, achieve my dreams, and make a positive impact on the world.

I also make sure to take care of myself spiritually, emotionally, and physically, so I can live a life full of joy and fulfillment.

There are several ways in which a person can become more resilient:

Here are some suggestions and topics to investigate (I have personally used/use them all and when coaching people).

Develop a positive mindset:

A positive mindset can help you see the good in every situation and think more optimistically. Focus on your strengths and believe in your ability to overcome challenges.

Nurture relationships:

Strong relationships with family and friends can provide a sense of security and support during difficult times. Cultivate relationships with people who are positive and supportive. Having such deep connections helps ground you and helps you tap into your deep well of resilience when needed.

Take care of yourself:

This includes getting enough sleep, maintaining a healthy diet and engaging in regular exercise. Taking care of your physical health can help you to maintain your mental and emotional well-being. The better your self-care routine the stronger your resilience foundation will be.

Practice mindfulness:

Mindfulness is the practice of being present and aware of your thoughts, feelings, and surroundings. Mindfulness can help you to manage stress and improve your ability to cope with difficult situations. It allows resilience to naturally flow to you.

Cultivate a sense of purpose:

Having a sense of purpose can provide motivation and direction, even in the face of adversity. Set goals for yourself and towards achieving them. Nothing builds resilience faster than getting outside your comfort zone.

Learn from experience:

Every difficult situation is an opportunity to learn and grow. Reflect on what you have learned from past challenges and use this knowledge to help you cope with future difficulties. See challenges as exercise for your resilience muscle.

Seek help when needed:

Resilience does not mean that you must go through difficult times alone. Reach out to family, friends, or a professional therapist for support when needed.

Resilience is a skill that can be developed and strengthened over time.

By focusing on developing a positive mindset, nurturing relationships, taking care of yourself, practicing mindfulness, cultivating a sense of purpose, learning from experience, and seeking help when needed, you can become more resilient and be better able to cope with whatever life throws your way.

Mini-Chapter Four: Post-Traumatic Growth & The New Me

Today, I am free of a life-threatening diagnosis and living a life that is full of purpose and meaning (core values).

Again, I'm not naïve and I know there are no guarantees in life (only that if you're born you will die someday), but my focus is not on what might happen because that will interfere too much and paralyze you.

My focus is on my mission in life - to be the best I can be for as long as possible (true quality of life/health-span not just lifespan) – to share my knowledge and wisdom with the world – to help and uplift – to give people hope.

My foundation is my family. Unfortunately, it looks like that's not a priority anymore in many western societies – and the children will pay the price. The most important foundation in your life is your family (place of origin/identity/I belong to this group/this culture/this area).

Cancer has transformed me from a fragile and vulnerable person to a resilient and strong individual (I´m still learning/it´s an ongoing process). It initiated a powerful personal journey of growth and strength that developed me on all fronts in life. I am grateful for the lessons I learned and the person I have become. I know that I can handle what life throws my way (I have a strong support system), and I am excited for the future.

As a cancer survivor, I can attest to the fact that the experience of battling cancer has taught me many valuable lessons about overcoming challenges and becoming a more resilient person. When I was first diagnosed with cancer, I was terrified. I had never faced such a serious health challenge before, and I didn't know how I was going to cope. But as my journey began, I quickly realized that I had to find a way to stay positive and keep moving forward (many of the cancer patients I´ve coached have experienced this).

One of the most important lessons I learned during my cancer journey was about the power of perseverance. This is an essential component of resilience, as it allowed me to bounce back from my diagnosis, and ultimately achieve my desired outcome (includes medical expertise but I did most of the hard lifting). Even when I felt like giving up due to being emotionally overwhelmed and low on energy, I kept pushing through the discomfort to get to the other side (I used visualization techniques as that works extremely well for me).

My family and ancestry have been an incredible source of resilience for me to draw on since the diagnosis.

I remember my maternal grandfather doing hard physical work in the forest and back home without ever complaining, I remember my father getting up in the middle of the night during summer to water the fields around the farm – because it was required for optimal results – he also never complained. They both did what was the right thing to do without the need for compliments and praise. Such role-models are just invaluable (my mother was also an integral and equally important and valuable part of the eco-system, as were my grandparents and great-grandparents/other family members – they helped form me during my childhood and teenage years).

My father also did well very in the military (as did his three older brothers) on the physical tests (top three among 90 soldiers) – I have used that in my visualization as well (some of that potential is in my DNA).

I also used every story I heard about our family members who participated in WW I and WW II.

It took some time to use these extreme examples as they would quickly overwhelm me emotionally, because I'm utterly impressed and in awe of those family members.

Two of them were captured, one in France and one in Russia, and in prison/labor camps and endured extreme hardship but managed to find their way home.

I used those examples in my visualization practice to become resistant to discomfort when training to or just above my comfort level (there are huge amounts of hidden resilience in such activities).

I applaud and salute everyone who participated in the World Wars and gave their best for what they believed in (values/traditions) to protect and serve (old-school heroism) - unfortunately tens of millions gave the ultimate sacrifice (every year I walk to a monument near the local church on Memorial Day to show my respect).

Their legacy lives on and they will never be forgotten (storytelling from generation to generation – inherited resilience – the will to live and overcome).

After I taught myself to properly tap into this source of resilience, I improved all my personal records by a large margin. It required a lot of mental and emotional energy and strength to find the optimal visualization frequency/intensity, but I was determined enough to complete the mission.

Perhaps the most transformative lesson I have learned from my cancer experience was the power of gratitude. Even on my darkest days, I tried to find something to be thankful for - whether it was the support of my loved ones, an act of kindness, or simply the fact that I was alive and doing my best. It takes resilience to keep going when you don´t feel like it. Gratitude helped me stay positive and hopeful, even in the face of tremendous adversity.

While the experience was undoubtedly difficult, it has taught me valuable lessons that have made me a stronger, more resilient person. Such as knowing that I can overcome most challenges (I´m capable on my own + support of a community if needed) that comes my way, and I am grateful for the opportunity to share my story and inspire others to persevere through their own struggles.

My mental prison cell where I had locked up shame, failures and guilt collected over decades had no more room – the lock and the chains could not handle more.

Through resilience I found the key and set all my trapped emotions free.

I began to practice mindfulness and self-care to properly deal with the chaos within, which helped me to stay grounded and to focus on the present moment. For years I had a habit of travelling back in time often, daily actually. If I could just change this or that (if I had done this/I could have done that), but here is the truth - you can't - so get over it and focus your attention on right now.

This is the most valuable sentence in my chapter/remember this:

Learn to live **with** your past, not **in** your past.

The past is for lessons – use those lessons and discard the rest.

"Regrets are reminders" – Jon Ch. Henningsen.

What matters is now – focus on the present moment – invest more and you'll be on your way to your desired destination. Everything will open up and expand (opportunities/possibilities) once your mindset has a gratitude-frequency/how can I serve and do good in the world? (you´ll be rewarded) This allowed me to accept my diagnosis and to move forward with a more resilient mindset.

You can practice the concepts I´ve mentioned in this chapter without a life-threatening disease or a major crisis, but the truth is most people postpone what they know they should work on. Without the cancer diagnosis I would not have broken a world-record in a back exercise called hyper-extension (for recreational lifters/we´re not talking elite-level/I lifted 110 kg x 3 reps./bodyweight that day 3rd of July 2020 = 91 kg), remember I had backpain for 20 years pre-diagnosis and the first couple of years after.

The Importance of a Positive Attitude and Support System

Having an optimistic mentality and a dependable support system can be exceedingly advantageous when addressing cancer. It can help to keep you motivated and focused on treatment and recovery.

Finding Meaning and Purpose in Life

When dealing with a cancer diagnosis or any other major crisis, it can be extremely difficult to find meaning and purpose in life.

Your purpose, mission, values and what makes life meaningful to you grounds you like an anchor on a ship in stormy weather.

Resilience is your mental anchor.

Strategies for Maintaining a Resilient Mindset

To maintain a resilient mindset, it is important to focus on the positive and find ways to stay connected to friends and family. It is also important to engage in activities that bring joy and to find ways to give back. Practicing mindfulness and self-care can also be beneficial for maintaining a resilient mindset (avoid feeling lost).

Finally, it is important to remember that there is hope and that it is possible to overcome adversity. When my doctor gave me the news that I had cancer, I was in shock. I had no idea what it meant or how I would be able to face it. I felt fragile, scared, and completely overwhelmed. I was not prepared for the roller coaster of emotions that awaited me on my journey with cancer. I found myself second-guessing every decision I made and questioning if I had the strength and courage to keep going.

Surprisingly, I found that those intense moments of challenge and adversity were the moments that forced me to grow and become more resilient and stronger than ever before.

From the lows came newfound strength and courage. The experience of being diagnosed with cancer transformed my mindset from fragile to resilient.

I developed a deep appreciation for life and the ability to find purpose and meaning in even the most trying times. My journey with cancer was also powerful and transformative on a personal level. Through treatment, I was able to gain greater clarity about who I am and the kind of life I want to lead. I learned to be fully present in every moment and use my struggles for personal growth. For example, I discovered the power of self-care and the importance of allowing myself to make mistakes and know that I can always find a way to move forward. I have also found the courage to reach out for help and build a strong support system.

Most importantly, I learned to focus on the present, value myself, and trust my inner strength. With this newfound resilience, I was able to take control of my life and navigate the difficult journey with cancer with courage, grace, and dignity.

I could not have done this without my wife, our daughter, my parents, my brother, my family, my wife's family and my best friends and clients (thank you for asking all those questions).

Thank you all for supporting me when I needed it the most!

My experience with cancer has taught me many lessons, but the greatest of these has been to trust my own personal strength and resilience. I am eternally grateful for my cancer journey, knowing that it has enabled me to develop on all fronts in life. I had so many questions about how this would affect my life, and I was filled with fear and uncertainty. But then something unexpected happened. As I faced my diagnosis, I began to develop a resilience that I hadn't known before. I became more confident in my own understanding of my condition and more open to talking about it. At the same time, I decided to take a proactive approach to my health and general well-being.

I incorporated several non-negotiable wellness practices into my daily routine. By taking control of my own health (the power of personal responsibility), I found strength and stability during the uncertainty of my diagnosis. And it had a ripple effect in my life:

I became more courageous in pursuing my goals, more confident in standing up for my beliefs, and more focused on building meaningful relationships.

The experience opened my eyes to my own inner power and set me on an inspiring journey of growth and development.

I'm grateful that I can use the lessons on my journey to inspire and motivate people in my gym and when I coach.

It has given me an appreciation for the small things in life, the courage to face challenges, and an understanding of my own worth as an individual. If you show up in life with the right attitude, you'll be rewarded in expected and unexpected ways.

"You have not lost everything, until you lose hope." - Jon Ch. Henningsen (I wrote this down in my journal after the first scan/ the first control visit post-diagnosis).

"Health is not everything, but without health, everything is nothing." - Arthur Schopenhauer/1788-1860 (this quote became a mental core-anchor for me on my health transformation journey).

Remember, forgiving yourself means letting go and moving on – let it go – do not live in your past for decades like I did (be warned – you´ll regret it).

As I tell my clients:

"Always do your best to be your best!"

"Always lead by example!"

“Resilience is very different than being numb. Resilience means you experience, you feel, you fail, you hurt. You fall. But, you keep going.”

~ Yasmin Mogahed

CHAPTER EIGHT

Cultivating Inner Resilience

By Inez Cooke

Introduction

It wasn't until I was offered this incredible opportunity to write this chapter that I realized just how resilient I've become in my life. I knew I had a lot to share about adversity, but I hadn't fully considered my innate resilience. To me, resilience means having continuous inner strength and vitality. In this chapter, I will show you how I've cultivated this over the past 18 months.

I'm not writing this for you to feel sorry for me; my aim is to illustrate the immense adversity I've overcome and the tools I've used to foster resilience and love myself completely. I hope to serve as an inspiration for you and that you, too, will recognize your own innate power of resilience.

In this chapter, I will share the tools I use daily to remain resilient and fully in tune with life. It's been a roller coaster journey, and it has shaped me into who I am today, and I wouldn't change any of it. I've been a seeker of inner peace most of my life since my university days reading numerous self-development books, joining spiritual communities, and following spiritual masters for three decades.

However, none of these masters or methods worked for me completely, although they all played their part in beneficial ways. I've been an emotionally sensitive person all my life with a nervous disposition devoid of any resilience! This was partly due to having the dyslexia label thrust upon me from a very early age, which meant you were 'thick' when I was a child. And this is what I perceived it to mean too, which has haunted me most of my adult life. But that is a story for another book! My other issue as a teenager going on into adulthood was that I had heavy menstrual cycles, so I became deficient in iron in my twenties, which led to feeling very tired, weak, paranoid, and dizzy. This is also a subject for another book! I had a lot to contend with from an early age.

Because of the dyslexia label, the only place where I didn't struggle was in the art department. I found resilience there. As I said, I've been searching for peace and resilience most of my adult life, but I couldn't find the tools to get me out of the hole I'd created. For most of my 20s and 30s, I'd spent most afternoons, two weeks in every month, in bed because I felt so paranoid and physically weak, mainly due to my menstrual cycles, although I didn't know this at the time, and I was too paranoid to go to the doctors for fear they would lock me up and throw away the key! I'm not joking; this is how I felt.

Before I can even remember, I found resilience in creating; from making art, painting pictures, and making imaginative worlds and games with my friends. I was never a bored child as I was always creating. Dreaming of being an artist and fashion designer.

My Resilience Awakening

As I sit here now at 49 years, I have undergone a self-development awakening in the last 18 months. I have discovered my own innate resilience. I have found the tools to get me out of the hole. I realized what I'd been doing to myself all my life, becoming a victim of my own mental and physical pain. I have often heard this phrase over many years in the self-development world.

'Thoughts create feelings,
And feelings create action and
how you create your own world'.

I'm sure you can relate to this too, but the missing part for me was how to get out of these thoughts and feelings so I could have innate resilience.

Yes, you can distract yourself with many methods, such as exercise, walking, jogging, or other activities to reset your nervous system and divert yourself from troubling thoughts and feelings. However, those thoughts will still be there; this doesn't get rid of them! For me, mastering my unhelpful thought loops has been a complete game changer in building resilience. Instead of falling victim to thought loops, a lot of them have now diminished so much that I barely notice them, or when thought loops arise, I observe them rather than engage in them. This has made me able to deal with being nervous and anxious and not take it so seriously!

When did the awakening begin?

In January 2022, I joined a Facebook group named 'The Ultimate Coach Facebook group.' I was invited to join by a man called named Martyn Dewes, whom I'd met on a retreat and held in high regard. His invitation led me to join the group, and I've never looked back!

This group is based on a book called *The Ultimate Coach* by Amy Hardison and Alan D Tompson.

This group is now known as the 'Being Movement' and has provided me with valuable tools. The coaches I've met through the book and the group have contributed significantly to my journey and the subject of resilience. I'll elaborate on this further in my chapter.

The book centers around the life and work of Steve Hardison. It's unique because you, as the reader, are prompted to read the back cover first, followed by the 'Before you begin' section situated at the beginning of the book. In the book, Steve Hardison encourages you to read as if you are the protagonist. Steve asserts that this is a book about being, and it's a book about you! To understand, you'll need to read the book for yourself; you will foster resilience in your own life by embodying the protagonist in the book. I highly recommend it, and each time I read it, I discover new things about myself. Additionally, the book offers some remarkable tools for cultivating resilience every day of your life. If you commit to using these tools, you'll find that your consciousness level and your inner resilience will rise.

This book has reshaped my perspective of myself and the world in an empowering, centered way. It led me to realize that I am neither defined by my past nor my future but by how I craft each present moment to create a wholly resilient and empowered life. From reading 'The Ultimate Coach' and participating in the Facebook group, I have encountered some phenomenal coaches. I have been coached by some of them over the past 18 months; among these are John Patrick Morgan, Matt Smith, Darren Farfan, and Sachin Sharma. Each coach has their unique style and practice, offering diverse ways to foster all your unique strengths, gifts, and talents and your innate resilience. While they may not explicitly reference resilience in their practices, it is what is inherently cultivated beneath it all for me, offering me a sense of intrinsic stability in life.

How have I developed to become mentally and emotionally resilient?

'The Work'

Some of the coaches I've worked with employ 'The Work' tools of Byron Katie, and I have found it incredibly helpful for myself. To go through these four questions with my coach to unravel the whirlwind of thoughts and beliefs whizzing around my mind since I was a child.

This practice is a form of meditation-- inviting you to dig deeply into your subconscious. Find a peaceful place where you won't be disturbed, allowing you to delve deeply into these questions with your inherent intuitive mind. Give this practice lots of time and space, as long as you need, so as to delve deeply into your subconscious. It may be necessary to revisit as far back as your early childhood and teenage years to uncover the triggers that shaped your behavior throughout your life. I used to believe my personality was set in stone from childhood or inherited from my parents. However, I've learned that my personality and being can evolve, and I don't have to think I'm stuck in ways of being like, 'I have an addictive personality, just like my father' or 'I find it difficult to apologize, like my mum.' These examples are fictional. Through this practice, you can be resilient in any situation, from somebody shouting at me to dealing with bullying and what type of love is needed in the present moment. This may mean I'm walking away, and I may not speak to that person again or not for some time! All actions should come from love to live a resilient life.

These are the four questions to go through and ask yourself. Please take your time; this is not an experience to rush. If you find yourself getting distracted, come back to it over days and weeks, however long is needed.

1. Is that thought true?
2. Can I know that it is absolutely true?
3. How does it make you feel when you think that thought?
4. Who would I be without that thought?
5. Then actively seek out the positive evidence in your life, no matter how small, where you are making changes through this work. Pay special attention to shifts in your mental processes, as these will evolve over time.

There are numerous YouTube videos on 'The Work' along with many books available for purchase and coaches in the Facebook group who use this tool. Thus, you are not alone if you wish to explore this method with a coach.

Engaging in this internal work helps untangle the thoughts racing around your mind. By undertaking this work, you'll find gradually and consistently, over time, the thought loops will gradually dissolve. Some thoughts and beliefs may take longer to shift than others. For me, I have found myself feeling exponentially more resilient in the past year and a half since I committed to doing 'The Work'!

This process can be used anytime you feel stressed, anxious, or overwhelmed. You will find fewer things that will bother you over time, so you won't need to do the practice as often. But new challenges will arise, and you have the tools to overcome them and be stronger in your resilience.

The Self-Forgiveness Work and Document

The practice of self-forgiveness is a tool Steve Hardison employs in his coaching. He uses 'the analogy the mind is like a GPS. 'You type in '1010 Arthur Street', it takes you to 1010 Arthur Street. Occasionally, there is a failure, but generally, GPSs are exceptionally accurate. Your mind is flawless. If you put in 'I'm amazing,' you get amazing. If you put in 'I'm afraid,' you get fear. If you put in 'I have extraordinary decision-making skill abilities,' that is what you get. Most people have plenty of crippling thoughts stored in their GPS. However, they are not etched in stone. 'And can be deleted over time.' -Quote taken from The Ultimate Coach Book P. 251. This captures the essence of this approach. Knowing that your thoughts and beliefs aren't etched in stone gives you a huge sense of relief and makes you know you are always resilient underneath the conscious mind.

Over time, depending on your commitment to the practice of self-forgiveness, you can dissolve negative, disempowering thoughts and beliefs. This fosters enduring resilience for the rest of your life, provided you continue this work.

1. Bring to mind an unfulfilled desire or call from inner wisdom.

2. Take note of what you feel about the unfulfilled desire and the limiting thoughts and feelings that come up.

3. Explore these limiting thoughts and write or voice record about these feelings. For instance, you might say, 'I am fearful of making a fool of myself.' Delve deep and express every limiting thought and feeling holding you back from your desire.

4. Then, one by one, liberate yourself from these limiting identities through a potent process of self-forgiveness. For example, 'I forgive myself for judging myself as arrogant.' Really feel the emotions coursing through your body and let them run their course. If you need to cry, you must; this is a great way of releasing your disempowering thoughts and beliefs forever. This process can be done again and again as many times as needed to release all your pent-up emotions.

After writing or vocalizing your forgiveness, listen for the deeper truth of your identity, which has been obscured by restrictive limiting identities. Without conscious thought, note down the words that spring from your intuition. You can write them in statements such as 'I am peace and calm in aggressive situations.'

5. Refine the resulting list of identity statements into approximately 10-20 powerful unique declarations of who you truly are!

This is what is referred to as a 'Document,' a declaration of your true self. Commit to reciting this as frequently as you can, memorizing it if possible. As your conscious frequency gets higher, your document will evolve also.

These questions are very loosely based on John Patrick Morgan's process of forgiveness; Matt Smith has a very similar yet unique approach.

'When you have a document inside of you, you get to the point where you are no longer arguing with yourself for your limitations; you start arguing with yourself for your greatness. It changes how you are in the world, and that, by extension, changes how the world interacts with you.'

Quote Karan Rai.

My Document

I am calm and still.
I am calm and present with what is.
I am love, and that is all there is.
I am that all my needs are met.
No one or thing is above or below me.
I am the healthiest woman in the world.
I am the wealthiest woman in the world.
I am that my cup is always overflowing.
I am endless amounts of time.
I am that I run the wealthiest art business on the planet.
I am community, and I make them everywhere I am in the world.
I am a powerful creator and create anything I desire.
I am focused on where I am and what I am doing.
I am that I feel the fear and do it anyway.
I am that anything is possible.
I am the best partner to my handsome, creative, loving, gentle, kind, funny, self-aware, and healthy boyfriend.
This is who I am, and my parents named me Inez, which means pure.

'Man never made any material as resilient as the human spirit. - Quote by Bern Williams.

If you don't commit to doing the inner forgiveness practice and skip straight to making a document or copying someone else's document, it won't work! I can confirm this because I've tried it! Steve Hardison would say, ' It's like putting sprinkles on a dog ship.' Need I say more?

These two practices can be done in conjunction with each other. Either one you feel drawn to accomplishing can be started first, or as I said, you can do them consecutively, whichever way works for you.

Here are some examples of how I've radically changed in this fairly recent time period from doing these two practices regularly and with support from my life coaches at times.

Being more relaxed in social situations, this could be a meeting at work or any kind of gathering from a dinner party or something larger. I would always have very negative thoughts and beliefs about why I shouldn't fit into these events; A lot of these have melted away, and when they do come up, I'm able to observe them and not be overwhelmed; As they would come in a flurry and sometimes, I would literally just run away, make my excuses and leave!

Getting stressed about the amount of work on my to-do list, which is quite a common one for most people. I have learned to stay more present and take one moment at a time and let intuition guide me through my day. Instead of my mad racing mind telling me, "You've got to wash the kitchen floor, then you have to do some gardening, then you've got to put a social media post up about your art business, then you've got to call a friend, and then you can do some artwork, which is supposed to be the main focus of the day!" I now tune in more to the intuitive, quiet voice in my head, which makes for a productive and peaceful day.

Meditation and Inner Resilience

Cultivating your focus and attention span is key to inherent resilience. Personally, I've had ADHD (attention deficit hyperactivity disorder) for many years. Firstly, through battling a mind labeled as dyslexic, which meant every thought went through the filter of 'I'm stupid.' In the last ten years, my concentration has gotten worse since having a smartphone, and I know a lot of people would identify with me with this. My ADHD mind means I think of 20 jobs to do at once; this, as you can imagine, is completely overwhelming and has left me paralyzed with what to do. I'm sure a snail is more productive in its day than I ever used to be!

Meditation can be an effective tool for improving your mental focus on the present moment rather than getting caught up in the past or worrying about the future. This practice can foster tremendous resilience by relaxing your mind, preventing it from racing incessantly and avoiding fixating on past or future events that may induce anxiety or stress. A calm, clear mind, always residing in the present moment, cultivates resilience. This state of mind is where intuition and wisdom reside, providing the best guidance. You can find and follow various meditation sessions on platforms like YouTube or other sources and gradually increase their length every so often to enhance your focus over time to an optimal amount of time that is right for you.

Alternatively, engaging in meditative activities such as arts and crafts, gardening, or even walking can also foster this focus. Doing them daily will help you increase your concentration, much like building muscle strength. As my coach Matt Smith would suggest, it's akin to lifting weights at the gym. You can't start with the heaviest weights on the first day. Instead, you need to build your strength gradually. The same principle applies to concentration and attention span. Regular practice is a prerequisite, just like everything in life, whether it's weight training or maintaining a calm and present mind.

This inner work has brought mental and emotional changes in me, dismantling many of the negative and self-defeating thought patterns that I have held for most of my life. As a result, I've become emotionally resilient, and I feel empowered to take on any challenge that comes my way.

Matt Smith often uses the analogy of our minds being like a garden. For it to stay looking beautiful, emotional weeding is necessary. When disempowering thoughts and beliefs surface, it's essential to confront them with 'The Work's Four Questions' and the self-forgiveness method. Over time you'll notice that the more you weed through doing the inner work, the less these thoughts and beliefs will affect you. They may still arise, but your heightened awareness will hear them and acknowledge them but not take them seriously, so the more you do the practices and meditation, the quicker they'll de-solve.

Another metaphor Matt uses is browsing in a bookshop. What area of the shop are you in, and what books are you looking at? Where are you putting your attention and focus in life?

I spent countless hours buying books and watching videos on how to eliminate issues. I can genuinely say this strategy has never worked for me! The more attention I gave the issue, the deeper I seemed to sink into it.

What Resilience Means to Me and How I Used it in My Life

Resilience, to me, signifies the ability to confront adversity with a sense of humor, to pick oneself up and restart, and to shower love and care on myself such that the love of others isn't a necessity for my wholeness and completeness in life. It implies establishing a profound connection with my intuition, allowing it to lead me through life, one moment at a time. Intuition, in my perspective, is the capacity to instinctively understand something without the need for deliberate reasoning. As a close friend described, "It's like an inner nagging," a subtle voice speaking to me. When I tune into this voice rather than my inner critic or my ego that keeps me safe, my life unfolds beautifully.

How Have I Become Resilient in My Life?

Over the past year and a half, my life and self-perspective have transformed beyond recognition. I transitioned from being somewhat agoraphobic and having minimal self-confidence in various aspects of my life, such as work, leisure, and intimate relationships. Determined to break free from my self-deprecation, I pledged to embark on the journey of inner work and strive to live the most resilient and fulfilling life. Today I'm resilient round the clock, thanks to the daily implementation of inner work and forgiveness practices in some form or another. This might simply mean being more attuned to my thoughts and what my inner critic is telling me. Rather than being judgmental about unwanted thoughts, I find myself saying, 'Oh, that's interesting,' observing them instead of plunging down a rabbit hole. This is a concept I picked up from my coach Matt Smith.

I follow through and commit, I do these practices as often as possible, whether it's engaging in inner work, meditating, or watching an enlightening video. I focus on it. Having a coach for most of the last 18 months has been beneficial as they've assisted me in navigating through my thoughts and realigning with my own intuitive guidance whenever I've felt lost.

My intuition serves as my resilience, present every moment of every day when I observe and recognize the learning opportunity they present. I can address these emotions on the spot in my day-to-day life or delve deeper into understanding them in my journal if needed. Now, I feel equipped to handle anything life throws at me. And you, too, can harness this 24/7 inner resilience, provided you commit to it and incorporate the practices into your life regularly.

How I Use My Painting to Stay Resilient

Throughout my life, engaging in artistic endeavors such as painting and drawing has bolstered my resilience. I find my haven in my studio, working on multiple paintings at the same time. Hours seem to fly by, feeling like minutes! When I encounter a stumbling block with a particular painting, I set it aside for a day or two and move on to another.

Creating art at this level transports me into a deep intuitive space, as a state of meditation nurtures my spirit and enhances my resilience for all other aspects of my life, as it puts me in a meditative space. There's an unexplainable joy in creating art purely for fun and for no reason other than the sheer delight it brings.

In between commissions, I like to come up with playful little art projects in sketchbooks to keep my creative styles loose and fresh. This also creates resilience in my creative soul.

As painting is quite a solitary affair, I've mentioned to a life coach friend that I'd love to create art with other people. Within a week, she had set up a small 'Creative Space' group on Zoom. This creative space is a small group that also likes to rely on their intuition for guidance, and we all support each other with our creative endeavors and our mindsets, which supports greater resilience in our lives.

'Art doesn't have to be perfect. It's the emotions you pour into it are the ones that must be REAL.' Verliza Gajeles

Conclusion

In summary, the journey towards developing inner resilience is challenging but always overall rewarding. Supported by a life coach, overcoming negative and overwhelming thoughts, and immersing myself in the world of deep meditation, has been a transformative and empowering process. By actively engaging in these practices, one can strengthen your resilience, thus equipping you with the best tools to navigate life's challenges with enhanced ease and grace.

Embarking on this inner work is a crucial component of fostering resilience. This journey entails self-reflection and the courage to face one's fears, limitations, and emotional patterns. By deeply exploring your internal landscape, you can gain a profound understanding of yourself, unearthing hidden treasures and resilience that may have previously been undiscovered. This heightened self-awareness facilitates targeted personal growth and transformation.

Neutralizing negative and unhelpful thoughts is an essential stride toward building inner resilience. Destructive, self-sabotaging thoughts can chip away at your confidence and your conscious vibration in the world and therefore impede your pleasure in life. However, by forgiving yourself and purely observing and saying to yourself, 'Oh, that's interesting' to the negative thoughts, rather than delving into them, they start to fade from your mind, leaving space for intuitive thought. The shifts in my beliefs and thinking have allowed me to meet setbacks and failures with resilience, seeing them as opportunities for learning and growth.

My creativity opens a potent channel for self-expression and emotional healing. Painting provides an avenue to connect with your deepest emotions, fostering a catharsis and release. Making art stimulates my imagination and contributes to bolstering my meditative resilience in complex and uncertain situations.

Ultimately, the journey towards inner resilience with 'The Work' and forgiveness tools and my continued immersion in art is a holistic approach that has empowered me to confront life's challenges with unwavering strength from trusting intuition. It is a continuous process of self-discovery and growth. By embracing this transformative journey, you can unlock your potential and cultivate a resilient spirit that supports you in all of life's dimensions.

"Pain teaches you what you need to fight for."

~ Sherri Mandell

CHAPTER NINE

Reclaiming Resilience

By Emily Kane

The pandemic and political disparities over recent years have taught us many things about our fitness to survive and thrive in a swiftly changing world. I realized that I needed to create methods to support my highest good and resiliency. Even now, it's impossible to imagine the challenges we would face with employment, limited access to goods and services, and within the healthcare system. During these recent turnabouts, I learned that although I had endured many trials and challenges, I was no longer the same person I had been—I was not as brave. Like many, I had experienced fluctuations in my strength and stamina, health, access to care, emotional toughness, and financial reserves. I felt the strain to remain optimistic and resilient. I was then reminded that I could not predict how things might flush out. This did not mean I should become apathetic, but I could intentionally shift my perspective and manage my feelings about what was happening.

Our ability to recover from events such as quarantine impacts our relationships and activities, and the stress of always wearing a mask can be highly disorienting. Still, resiliency is dynamic and achievable when we develop a practice of self-care. Tapping into our innermost self can be a powerful tool in creating resilience because we often become what we tell ourselves we are, but normally with negative self-talk such as "I am not worthy" of something. We tend to believe the stories we echo to the point of them becoming self-fulfilling. In overwhelming moments, our initial reaction may be to deny or resist that the calamity is real or lasting. However, by developing new patterns of thinking, feeling, and reacting, we can limit the intensity of the jolt.

Our investments toward our mental, emotional, physical, and spiritual constitutions create the potential for balance between chaos and arriving at solutions. The subconscious mind runs on autopilot to the scripts we employ. When we express gratitude for the people and things that we have in our lives, it generates a sense of calm whereas focusing on forced isolation would perpetuate fear and anxiety. Therefore, resilience isn't just about enduring life's challenges but actively participating in creating our narratives. It's a practice that involves self-awareness, self-care, and the deliberate cultivation of positive beliefs. By recognizing the transformative power of our inner dialogue, we empower ourselves to become more resilient individuals, capable of weathering life's storms and shaping our destinies with strength and purpose.

As children, our senses evolve to teach us how to adjust and adapt to the world. We are not trained to raise our energetic vibrations; instead, we are taught compliance for safety and adherence to societal norms, which is why we initially resist change. One of the first communication tools we understand is the energy or vibration around the expression of words. The tone in which words are used can tell our minds how to feel regardless of how we speak to ourselves, others, or how we listen to others talk around us, i.e., a child being admonished, an angry partner, negative self-talk, or the evening news.

In discovering who we are destined to become, there are lessons to be learned along the way. Our capacity to build resilience is much like any muscle we want to get stronger; first, we must exercise it to create its potential, then continue exercising it to realize its fullest. When we fail and fail again, our experiences teach us to master that, which has once made us feel defeated or conversely limit our reach out of fear of failing again. I was a single parent in the military for 15 years and during that time, our country witnessed global terrorism, anthrax, Severe Respiratory Acute Syndrome (SARS), and the bombing of the USS Cole (DDG-67) while I was deployed on a ship abroad. These experiences put me through the spectrum of self-doubt to confidence and clarity so often that I thought I could handle anything.

Inherent to all of us is a burning desire to realize our distinctiveness. However, there are also peripheral influences that we have come to rely on to cultivate our self-esteem, sense of peace, and belonging while creating a fear of the unknown. We are members of a family, a workplace, a spiritual organization—in many ways, we have learned to modify our pieces to fit into the greater puzzle. We have learned the language and behaviors of our people, including some not-so-desirable traits.

For decades, I have served in an organization that had strongly influenced my understanding of myself and the world around me. I believed I had established boundaries between my aspirations and my role as a team player. When I recognized that I had gotten lost in the depths of chaos of the world around me, I had to learn how to begin again and restructure aspects of my resiliency. Achieving this was difficult because I had to reconnect to myself and learn how to elevate my vibration from a group thinking pattern to define my singular strengths and weaknesses.

I had formerly relied on the guidance of others to adapt and overcome, but those resources were no longer available to me since I moved from overseas to an unfamiliar state and retired from the military. Nevertheless, in these times of adversity, I could take heart that although things were not stabilizing, I was able to acquire new skills, routines, and networks to begin again. A fundamental key to overcoming hardships is resilience. Sometimes, we prevail only through grace; other times, we find transformative solutions and a sense of connection from our shared experiences. Perhaps this is why I have consciously considered what I use for my sense validation. Even in the most dysfunctional situations, when change occurred, my ability to recover from conflict and uncertainty was also impacted. The comfort and reassurance I once enjoyed in belonging no longer supported thriving in today's world.

At its core, resilience is not a one-size-fits-all concept but a deeply personal journey. It starts with the realization that the path everyone seems to be following is, in fact, exclusive to the individual. Embracing our uniqueness becomes a pivotal step in the process of building resilience.

Our distinct perspectives and life journeys shape our experiences of pain, joy, and sorrow. It's essential to acknowledge that we can never fully comprehend the depth and endurance of another person's reality solely because we may have encountered similar experiences or emotions. Furthermore, even within ourselves, our emotional responses vary based on the circumstances. Recognizing our natural patterns and reactions to life's events enables us to develop responses that can mitigate or diffuse their impact.

Delving into our emotional states provides valuable insights that can be harnessed to manage the effects of lower vibrational energy. As we adjust our thoughts, we can simulate desired emotional outcomes or, at the very least, diminish the most detrimental aspects of lower vibrational energy by elevating them into higher vibrational energies.

Albert Einstein's profound insight that "everything in life is vibration" underscores the interconnectedness of everything in our world. Much like physical objects, emotions, thoughts, and beliefs emanate vibrational frequencies. The higher the vibration, the lighter, happier, and more joyful our experiences become. Conversely, lower vibrations bring about feelings of density, anger, or resentment.

Our vibrational energy shapes our reality, attracting outcomes that resonate with our emotional frequencies. Resilience, then, involves acknowledging our uniqueness and taking charge of our thought patterns and emotional responses to elevate our vibrations. By doing so, we align ourselves with positive energies that empower us to navigate life's challenges with greater strength and grace, making resilience a dynamic and transformative force.

In learning to give myself compassion and care, I increased my capacity to hold space for those around me. I did not realize, at the time, that prayer, working out, and reflections of gratitude were considered self-care. I have always been a work in progress because self-care is an ongoing practice, and one solution cannot solve all areas of necessity in perpetuity. For decades, I had used brain hemispheric synchronization (hemi-sync), soundscapes, frequencies, and visualizations to manifest higher energetic vibrations and focus on desired outcomes. I started using these techniques as instruments that I could use in place of meditation to enhance my peace and harmony. It has long been believed that hemi-sync has the potential to improve cognitive functions, reduce stress and pain, increase memory abilities, and enhance creativity and decision-making.

Creating resilience is about redirecting our attention from fear and doubt toward hope and positivity. The conscious mind can only effectively focus in one direction at a time. When focusing on fear, it is unlikely to create a positive result. It may even be interfering with one's potential to increase their resilience. When focusing on beneficial outcomes, there will be affirming patterns at work supporting that mentality. The mind is so powerful that we can generate our ability to overcome fears and limiting beliefs. Subconsciously, thoughts do not question, correct, or analyze, so when we speak loving and encouraging words, they can make those words a reality.

Intuiting how our body typically feels and then any discerning changes, physically or mentally, helps reveal what is subconsciously occurring beneath the surface by how it presents itself. The mind-body connection influences our biochemistry and nervous system (electrical) responses. Additionally, by practicing self-care, we can initiate desired outcomes. For example, there are common references that link stress with cortisol levels and the development of visceral fat around the belly; physiological and hormonal "fight or flight" responses to potential danger; and the production of endorphins and dopamine when we exercise and sleep soundly. Incorporating self-care routines helps us to build resiliency by perceiving and addressing what is happening within our mind and body, nurturing positive thoughts and actions, and fortifying our overall well-being.

Furthermore, being tuned to our bodies and noticing which activities or circumstances generate biochemical reactions enable us to pause and evaluate situations for a root cause. As with any animal, we are born with inherent survival instincts. When we ask ourselves why we feel a certain way, we may not fully understand why we have these questions. Our bodies are wired to "sound the alarm" and alert us when something doesn't feel good or normal.

There was a time when I was frequently and inappropriately confronted with hostility from someone I thought was a friend. I noticed an increased tightening in my shoulders and neck. I had been waiting patiently, or so I thought, to receive help with a project that had been put off for several weeks and now was becoming imminent. I realized that by trying not to be bothersome, I was consequently not forthcoming to them about how the situation made me feel. I was not honoring myself, which began to create physical discomfort. Despite being mindful of my words and thoughts, I was not transparent about my feelings because I didn't want to create conflict. Realizing that I was not communicating all my feelings lowered my vibration in the area of my throat and manifested into a sore throat.

It is not easy to take a breath and convert a negative thought into a corresponding positive one. Every action has a correlating reaction, just as every cause has some effect, and every effect has a cause. Hence, to change the effect, we must change the underlying meanings assigned to those thoughts to expand our resiliency. We can quickly understand how the experience activates empowering, higher vibrational energies by changing our ideas and perspectives. Consequently, this shift inspired me to delve beyond feelings into my role in this confusing development. As I examined why I felt perplexed and betrayed, I noted that I had initially felt excited about the opportunity to have help. I could already feel the joy building in me when I imagined how it would be when the project was finished. Later, I felt sad and deceived.

It did not take long before I realized I had created that energy around agreements destined to falter under the weight of reality. Their truth existed before I became part of their dynamic, and I had expectations that I had developed from what was presented as a best-case scenario. Yet, the people involved had their energies around an agenda they brought into the situation. We had not coordinated a solid foundation for a mutually beneficial outcome. In addition to examining the cause and effect, I was struck by the impact of reality and the aftermath of failing to have realistic hopes. I had compromised my resilience. I did not have authority over their time, intentions, or norms; I could only understand the emotions I tied to what was desired and seemed possible to me. Conversely, they did not consider how their decisions impacted me because they were entrenched in what affected them.

When I could identify what I was feeling, I could then address it by taking steps to raise energetic support for myself and resilience to my emotional mind-body connection. I learned that when we fail to honor ourselves, we essentially tell ourselves that we don't deserve as much consideration as others. We cannot afford to constrain who we are or what we need because of how it may make someone else feel—we must witness how it makes us feel. I am not condoning selfishness to the exclusion of others, but to actively advocate for our most benevolent outcomes while being genuine to ourselves.

Resiliency is a profound journey of self-awareness, compassion, and the development of our overall endurance. Realizing our intrinsic value liberates us to make choices more aligned with empowering ourselves. The journey is our own; while we may traverse this path together, we all deserve to feel loved and valued regardless of our differences. It is through our willingness to examine our beliefs, let go of paradigms that no longer serve us, and design a life with meaning and purpose. Our experiences enable us to recognize methods we can use to restore balance amid overwhelming experiences and protect our boundaries. Furthermore, we understand that resilience can manifest as a compassionate presence. Even when we cannot ease the pain of others, we can witness the seeds of resilience taking root, empowering us to weather the storms of transformation and flourish in whatever lies ahead.

Resilience is intricately linked to our relationships' quality and commitment to authenticity. As adults, forging connections with like-minded people can be challenging. However, what truly matters is the connection, the profound understanding that we don't necessarily need to share identical beliefs to respect and learn from one another.

Within my circle of friends, a remarkable example of how being valued and accepted for who I am nurtures my resilience. One friend stands out, encouraging me to embrace my true self without apologizing. It mirrors the age-old "golden rule"—treating others as we wish to be treated. This liberating approach to communication allows us to share our experiences and ideas with honesty and transparency. Simultaneously, we share an unspoken understanding that we need not lay our life stories on the table for scrutiny; some things will naturally reveal themselves over time.

Our relationship is firmly grounded in transparency, honesty, and acceptance. By approaching relationships this way, we eliminate uncertainty about each other's intentions and reduce confusion about expectations. We recognize that each of us is a unique creation with a distinct purpose. Furthermore, by demonstrating self-love and self-honor, we convey our respect for one another.

Keeping our truths present in our interactions fosters a deeper sense of fairness. It creates a space where our authentic messages can be integrated and understood. We don't need all the answers to every question, but we need to trust our decision-making processes. This wisdom is precious because our life journeys are laced with lessons that shape us and help us heal as we evolve into the individuals we are meant to become.

Creating resilience is intrinsically tied to our unwavering commitment to facing and embracing the truth. This commitment forms the sturdy foundation of our inner strength. Prioritizing the presence of truth in our lives allows us to navigate challenges, adapt to circumstances, and critically evaluate the messages we encounter. Through these authentic connections and a commitment to honesty, we find the resilience to thrive in a world filled with uncertainty and possibility.

Choices are part of our evolutionary growth into finding purpose. We are empowered to negotiate which meanings we apply to everything in our existence and how much those meanings impact our emotional wellbeing is very personal and unique. Attitude has a significant impact on how we perceive any given situation. Far too often, when events feel beyond our control, we relinquish power to justify becoming apathetic. I can choose my path and response, thereby creating my resilience. I am reminded that the sun doesn't always shine, but when it does, I can almost feel the energy exuding from our fingertips. This is a time when I take advantage of my vitality and enthusiasm. Yet, when the moon reveals itself, I am reminded to rest and recover.

Resilience is a dynamic dance with life's ever-changing rhythms, a journey that often frustrates us with societal pressures urging conformity in our beliefs and behaviors. Society seems to suggest that belonging requires uniformity in ideals, patterns, and beliefs, making it challenging to maintain high energy levels when we must acknowledge and accept life's natural ebbs and flows.

In my quest for resilience, I've discovered a valuable technique: aligning the start of projects with my natural rhythmic ups and downs while minimizing exposure to negativity. When I sense myself vibrating at a lower frequency, I create a protective cocoon to introspect and understand the root causes of my emotions. I refrain from imposing my emotional state on others, even though I know their presence could potentially elevate my energy. It's a practice that centers around positive thinking, expressing gratitude, vocalizing affirmations, and acting with kindness. These habits enable me to sustain or recover my energetic vitality over time.

Resilience is deeply intertwined with our ability to manage and transform the overflowing emotions that life can bring. The phrase "my cup runneth over," often associated with joy and abundance, can equally be applied to the overwhelming anxiety and the erosion of our capacity to adapt when adversity strikes.

In addition to the pandemic, I took care of an elderly family member during their last years. That made me realize that despite my reservoir of compassion and love, there are moments when someone else's pain surpasses my capacity to enact substantial change. In these humbling instances, I've understood the importance of expressing my joy and abundance. Through this self-care and self-expression, I can be at my best, offering a stabilizing presence for those grappling with low-vibrational experiences.

In many ways, it's akin to being a dry sponge in the presence of a saturated one. Just as the dry sponge absorbs and eases the excess water, I aim to alleviate the emotional burdens of those I care for. Providing solace and support while recognizing the limits of my influence is an integral aspect of resilience.

I recently began morning breathing exercises and checking in with my body. I sit mindfully tuning into how my body feels—did I sleep restfully or dream? Do I desire to pursue an activity (stretching, walking, or writing)? Is there a thought that I keep thinking? The more validation I give myself, the stronger the imprint resonates. After I tune in, I like to say at least five things that I am grateful for because the energy around gratitude attracts more things to be thankful for or lends toward being grateful for what I already have, such as family, friends, a job, etc. Simple reflections of gratitude are potent in building resilience.

Then I like to finish my practice with "I am" affirmations about whatever I want to support, such as, "I am in optimal health; I am creating a life that I love; or I am unstoppable, and there is always a solution to every problem." This is when I set the tone for my day by speaking it into existence. By beginning each day with this intentional practice, we attract more positivity into our lives and empower ourselves to face adversity with a fortified spirit and unwavering determination. It's the foundation upon which we build our resilience, one grateful thought and affirmative statement at a time.

I discovered that when I could not focus on my daily regimen, I felt disoriented and emotionally out of balance. When I was not focused on caring for myself, it became obvious to the people around me. Since resuming, I have begun incorporating emotions, senses, and the experiences of attaining what I manifest. What helps is finding a place free from noise or outside distractions so that I can be mindful of what I allow to influence my thoughts. I have a place where I sit comfortably and listen to my quietness. I take a few moments to settle in and quiet my inner chatter. During this time, I listen to my inner wisdom. By consciously bringing awareness to our energetic state to understand what our body is conveying, we can learn to manage the resiliency we need during that time.

Resilience is the ability of the human spirit to heal, grow, and overcome adversity by creating positive energy. We must practice raising our energetic vibrations through affirming thoughts, actions, and feelings. Building resilience requires that we possess a belief in our worthiness and honor those aspects that are intensely our own. When we are around others, they may help us to vibrate at a higher frequency as a collective, but ultimately, it is our body, and we must give it what is necessary to thrive and surmount obstacles.

Resilience is not about having all the answers to life's questions but rather about having faith in our decision-making process. It's the understanding that we may not know everything, but we can trust our ability to navigate challenges with integrity and authenticity. This trust is a wellspring of resilience, enabling us to confront adversity with a steadfast spirit. The analogy of coal becoming a diamond reminds us that resilience is not about avoiding pressure but about embracing it as a catalyst for personal growth. It underscores the idea that we can shine brilliantly through life's challenges, just like a diamond forged in the depths of the earth. Much like the diamond, resilience emerges from the depths of our experiences, where we confront difficulties, hardships, and uncertainties. These trials, although demanding, have the potential to bring out our inner brilliance, strength, and resilience. They push us to adapt, learn, and grow, just as the coal's transformation creates something beautiful and enduring.

“Resilience is the capacity of a system, enterprise, or person to maintain its core purpose and integrity in the face of dramatically changed circumstance.”

~ Andrew Zollli

CHAPTER TEN

How Nepalese Society Portrayed Resilience after the Earthquake in 2015

By Sagar Bahadur Dhakal

"Resilience" was a much-headlined word across all media in Nepal during the Earthquake of 2015.

"Does Nepalese society have the resilience to overcome this catastrophe?" This was the pressing question posed by local newspapers. From the first two weeks when it was all chaos, to the months where I actively took part in organizing relief and support together with the NGO my mom had set up in 2007, to the years where we completed rebuilding many houses and a health center, I saw not just individuals but also communities transforming through different phases. These different phases are the keys to creating resilience. Just like when a baby is born, he goes through various stages before he turns into a mature adult, resilience is built up with the series of phases individuals and communities go through.

The intention of producing this chapter is so that people can be inspired by the resilience exhibited by individuals and society and, at times of need, be able to choose between being heroic, being selfless, accepting sacrifices, developing endurance to face the struggle and rebuild themselves and their society.

Heroism

It was a busy Saturday. A group from a firm visited our NGO (orphanage), where we had 40 children under our residential support. After the program was over, we moved the chairs inside the kitchen from outside, where there was a small space to conduct the program, and it happened. The sound was akin to a thousand trees falling at once, growing rapidly closer. Pretty soon, you realize it's there, and you feel something is out of balance; you are out of balance. As you look around, you see the top of the buildings shaking here and there. You could hear the frantic clamor of panic pervading, and although we had always experienced small quakes every year or so, nothing was comparable to this one.

I could somehow feel the disaster approaching with the sounds of havoc, the screams, and vibrations. It wasn't really a conscious act but more of an instinctive reaction to rush for the safety of the children inside the building. Those who were outside were already hugging us in their arms, overwhelmed with apprehension and fear. My immediate reaction was to run inside the main door of the building to where the stairs began. "Everyone down now, there's an earthquake," I shouted repeatedly while the remaining ones came out. I led them through an alleyway to the main road, which felt safe.

It was 7.8 magnitude on the Richter scale. The epicenter was below Barpark, a village 140 km away from Pokhara and our orphanage. It was completely destroyed, with no houses left standing. Generally, the homes in villages are made of mud and rocks with stone roofs. As for the day's timetable in the village, since it was a Saturday afternoon, it was time for people in the houses to rest inside after their morning work in the fields. While everyone expected similar powerful aftershocks, little did anyone know that we would live in a state where we experienced quakes every hour or so every day for the next few months. The first three days were very confusing. There were hourly tremors, all forms of communication were down, and rumors like the falling of "Dharahara," a nine-story historical tower in Kathmandu, and many other historical sites. There was no official circular or statement from the government yet.

The next day, I was at the insurance office. A few weeks ago, four of the goats from our farm were lost in the forest, and the next day, we found leftovers from dismembered body parts, possibly attacked by some wild animal like a leopard. Because of the frequent earthquakes that had occurred every hour or so, we knew offices and businesses would close down for some time, so we contacted the agent to submit the documents we had already compiled before everything closed down. While quakes were coming now and then, I couldn't help but notice the cracked beam in the veranda where the stairs led to the office's entrance on the third floor. As I submitted the documents, it happened again.

In that tumultuous moment, as the urgency of the shouting, "Run, run, run!" echoed through the air, resilience unfurled its wings among us. Amidst the chaos, instinct took over, propelling everyone toward the small door, a path to safety. Like a symphony of movement, we surged through the narrow staircase, descending to the ground floor, a collective determination pushing us forward.

Behind the building's sheltering walls lay an expanse of open space, a sanctuary of respite from the looming threat. The building's design, a blend of foresight and necessity, offered solace as we regrouped, each of us seeking refuge and gathering strength in the shared understanding that together, we were stronger.

Amid this urgent exodus, my gaze alighted upon the last figure to emerge from the stairwell, the same voice that had pierced the air with the call to flee. As my eyes met him, a quiet recognition bloomed within me. In his eyes, I glimpsed a reflection of the same resolute responsibility that had guided my actions, a silent testimony to the resilience woven into our human fabric.

It was a poignant moment that would linger in the corridors of my memory, a touchstone for introspection. The urgency of the situation had spotlighted the spectrum of our choices: the instance when altruism outweighed self-preservation and this very moment when survival took precedence. The dichotomy of these responses carved a groove of contemplation in my thoughts, a reminder of the intricate dance between our innate desire to safeguard others and the instinctual need to protect ourselves.

Resilience seemed to be a symphony with ever-shifting notes—a balance between the impulse to stand steadfast for others and the necessity to preserve one's well-being. In that narrow window, we had each written a verse of this intricate composition, etching our actions into the annals of experience. Looking around at faces carved with both resolve and vulnerability, I recognized that within this chaos, the seeds of resilience had taken root, knitting us together in a shared narrative of survival and strength.

Eventually, in the next three days, communication began to start again, and the flow of information through different channels reported the level of devastation that occurred. On the second day, it began to rain heavily for a week. The TV showed the rubble where tall buildings had once stood in urban areas, and the villages that now don't have houses anymore. Police, army, and volunteers were all busy clearing the rubble and saving anyone trapped. Not to mention, there were also the frequent casualties of those who were trying to save others. Many service members would get trapped themselves and die amidst the rescue efforts. As we watched on the TV, the servicemen went on rescue missions, breaking the rubble of buildings one after another in the week-long rain, their tears reminding them of the devastation of their houses and families.

Local leaders and organizations nationwide started initiating relief support even when living in temporary shelters in open fields. It was evident that the people themselves had to stand up. While the houses were open and people were still living in temporary shelters with constant fear, they started donating what they could. Tents, rice, food grains, soap and daily essentials, and medical items were then collected by many organizations, and some volunteered to take them to the villages destroyed by epicenters.

In the crucible of adversity, resilience emerged as a beacon of hope, casting its transformative light upon each individual. The call to rise above personal anguish and embrace heroism echoed through the air, igniting a collective awakening. As eyes beheld the widespread devastation, a shared understanding took root—a realization that our burdens, though heavy, were woven into a larger tapestry of communal suffering. In this pivotal juncture, the fulcrum of our response was the very essence of resilience.

In the middle of the catastrophe, we became the architects of our resilience, sculpting it from the clay of determination and unity. The resonance of selflessness echoed through our actions, forging bonds that transcended individual boundaries. With each selfless act, we fortified the foundation of our collective strength, and the concept of heroism evolved from the exceptional to the communal.

Sacrifices and Losses

In the middle of crises, sacrifices and losses emerge as a stark reality, woven intricately into every life affected. Amidst the chaos and upheaval, the tendrils of devastation reach deep, touching lives in ways unforeseen. For instance, the earthquake's unrelenting force carved a painful chasm in my own experience—a beloved figure, my cousin's uncle, became entwined with the avalanche's remorseless embrace.

This gentle soul had been a beacon of kindness, extending a helping hand to my family during a pivotal juncture when I ventured to Kathmandu for my engineering studies. His loss, a poignant reminder of the fragility of existence, cut through our hopes and optimism, leaving us grappling with the weight of an irreversible absence. In the initial hours, buoyed by the flicker of hope, we clung to the belief that communication might have faltered, and rescue might be forthcoming. We prayed for a miracle in that hushed space between despair and hope.

Yet, as days turned into a procession of uncertainty, the hard truths became apparent. Encounters with others who had crossed paths with the ill-fated group chiseled away at the façade of optimism. Those who had been the last to witness their presence painted a somber picture—a portrait of finality etched into their accounts. It was a chilling testimony of the earthquake's indiscriminate wrath, as if the forces of nature had chosen Langtang as their canvas for devastation.

In Langtang's embrace, a village lay entombed beneath an avalanche, a scene of heartbreaking calamity. It stood as a stark testament to the capricious nature of fate, a reminder that resilience was born from surviving the tempest and enduring the aftermath. In the tapestry of tragedy woven by the earthquake's impact, many shared similar fates—families sundered, homes erased, and lives forever altered.

Amidst these tales of loss and sorrow, resilience emerged not as a mere buzzword but as a lifeline. It was the thread connecting survivors, binding their experiences in a common narrative of strength and healing. As the collective heart of a nation grieved, this resilience emerged as an unwavering commitment to rebuild, honor the memory of those lost, and forge a future from the ashes of despair.

Sacrifices and losses, though painful, stand as the crucible from which resilience is forged. In the face of adversity's unrelenting onslaught, communities and individuals discover within themselves the latent capacity to endure, heal, and rebuild. In these moments of raw vulnerability, the true essence of resilience emerges—a testament to the human spirit's capacity to rise, undaunted, from the depths of tragedy.

It was about two weeks since the first quake and the regular aftershocks were happening each hour. Two major aftershocks of 6.7 and 7.3 magnitude caused more devastation. We lived in the vegetable garden we had rented near the orphanage that had enough open space for a week. Even during such a time, my mom had been visiting shops and buying tents, food grains, soap, and other daily essential goods that she could take to areas that needed help.

Suraj was a boy from Gorkha who had lived with us. Like his father, he also had some psychological illness and struggled at school. We helped him get treatment, and he's still on his medicine. His village was the next hill from Barpark, and we wondered how the conditions there were. Most of the houses were destroyed at the epicenter of the major quake, and people were living in the fields, whether they had tents or not, out in the rain.

We went to his village with a few members of our organization. It was quite an adventure. Five of us were in a pickup truck full of relief support. Every hour or so, another quake hit, and we had to stop, sometimes staying in the vehicle and running away from the truck if the road was on top of a cliff. Once the highway was over, we took the mountain road, and doing so started giving us the chills. The quakes caused the soil and stones to drop from the mountains onto the roads, so there was no chance of getting out. There was a time when the ground was shaking, and soil began pouring down the side, so despite the quake, we rushed our vehicles forward. As we got closer along the way, we witnessed the scale of damage getting even worse. It was literally like heading into the abyss. Every village we saw had destroyed houses in it. People would watch us, hoping the relief was for them.

Amidst the chaos that followed the disaster, our unwavering determination led us to his village by evening's descent, our hunger forgotten in the face of urgency. The earth beneath our feet bore the scars of upheaval, its fault lines weaving through fields that had once known tranquility. Our mission was clear—after assessing the damage that had befallen Suraj and his father, we distributed tents and essentials, a small beacon of relief amidst the ruins. Time was a luxury we couldn't afford, for the needs were vast, and the night held a sky brimming with uncertainty.

A school, once a sanctuary of education, now stood transformed into an open expanse—a canvas of hope marked by rubble and shards. Here, we gathered, driven by a common purpose—delivering tents and supplies to those whose lives had been upended by fate's capricious hand. The scars etched into the landscape were echoed by the hollow spaces in our hearts, the classrooms now shadows of the lives they had once held.

As we navigated the logistics of distribution, a symphony of resilience unfolded. Volunteers, whose lives had been forever altered, stood shoulder to shoulder, their hands extended to help others before themselves. A new kind of architecture was being erected within the ruins—one of unity, empathy, and shared purpose.

Amidst the swelling tide of people, the scene seemed chaotic. But from the midst of the crowd, a remarkable transformation had taken place. Volunteers, rising from within the community, became architects of order. They organized the people, stratifying them by age and need, transforming the scene from disarray to cohesion.

Among the volunteers, I witnessed the embodiment of resilience. There were individuals who, despite having lost their own homes, perhaps even their own families, stood resolute in the face of adversity. They had transmuted their grief into a powerful force that propelled them to provide for others, alleviate suffering where they could, and ensure the vulnerable were not left behind.

The school's hallways may have crumbled, but from within the rubble arose something far more enduring—community, compassion, and an unwavering commitment to collective healing. In that moment, the essence of resilience revealed itself. It was not just the ability to endure but the power to rise, mend, and uplift others even when one's foundations were shaken.

Thus, sacrifices and losses at such times are something no one can escape. Once the losses are incurred, it's better to accept them and move on because there is nothing we can do about it, but many things can be done about the present and the future. Accepting losses and sacrifices plays a vital role in creating resilience. Sacrifices and losses enable one to harness the inner qualities of a person. Actions harmonize in the beat of pain and suffering. Acts for today help us to accept reality and live in the present, the new reality that allows us to respond to the ever-changing demands of the present, thus nurturing the vital components of resilience.

Resilience Amidst Ruins

In the following months, our organization did many other relief distribution programs, visiting more epicenter areas like Sindhupalchowk and taking relief to other villages and indigenous communities. Another memorable trip for me was the trip to the Chepang community.

Chepang, with its rich ancestral history, stands as one of the most underdeveloped ethnic communities in Nepal. They still forage in the forest for food, living completely off the land. We were informed about this community, particularly in a remote location, by a local leader residing in the nearest village. After five grueling hours on the rugged paths towards the highway, we had to turn right and go up and down the hills until the evening. Their settlement was inaccessible by road, so they gathered at the nearest village. This time, we had a health worker with us, so we were also able to do basic checkups with essential medicines. It was summertime, so we also brought them mosquito nets as diseases were spreading through the mosquito bites. No one had proper clothes, and their average body structure was smaller than most. Because of the earthquake, their houses which were made of mud and sticks were completely destroyed. Luckily, we had more tents.

A group of government officers and local leaders helped us manage the aid.

Having faced the challenges of living in the fields, battling exhaustion, and the ever-present uncertainty, I felt that my hardships paled in comparison to the living conditions they were going through. While the communities in villages and cities were having difficulties due to the shortage of fuel, food, and other essentials, this particular Chepang community was living in some of the worst conditions. These people were living in primitive ways and used a language only few would understand. Because it was remote and inaccessible, no one had ever visited them with relief. Later on, their circumstances were highlighted in the national newspaper, and many other teams also visited them. The experience has taught me resilience is also about adaptability, a positive mindset, resourcefulness, humility, and finding joy in simplicity. These lessons underscore that resilience is a dynamic and holistic quality that encompasses various aspects of human experience, and it can be found in the most unexpected places and circumstances.

My mother's journey through life was a testament to resilience, a quality deeply ingrained within her from a young age. Despite her challenges, such as leaving school to care for her numerous siblings, she possessed an unwavering drive to make a difference. Her determination led her to actively engage in various community organizations supporting the underprivileged.

Our family's humble beginnings, living in a mud house nestled amidst a cornfield, only highlighted the resilience that coursed through her veins. Every evening, when darkness enveloped our village, my mother embarked on a 25-minute trek to deliver food to my father, who managed a shop. In those moments when the lights faded, and my cries pierced the quiet night, I realized that her resilience was not just a quality but a lifeline. I would call out for her, "Mummy, mummy," incessantly, until I heard her reassuring voice, or a caring neighbor came to comfort me.

Even when I entered the world of formal education, my mother's commitment to resilience remained unshaken. She continued to dedicate herself to establishing community organizations focused on the welfare of children and women. Each morning, our home became a hub of activity as people sought her out for guidance and support in resolving various challenges.

Through her unwavering determination and commitment to others, my mother embodied the essence of resilience, demonstrating that in the face of adversity, one can endure and thrive, uplifting those around them with their indomitable spirit.

My mother continued on a remarkable journey of resilience throughout my high school years, which began in 2007. It all started when she established an orphanage, and in the years that followed, she initiated a handicraft industry aimed at empowering marginalized women. The inception of the orphanage was not without its challenges; in its first year, my mother incurred a substantial debt of $9,000. However, her unwavering determination and resilience soon became evident as she worked tirelessly to ensure the project's sustainability.

I often find myself in awe of where she draws her boundless energy. Despite the numerous obstacles and struggles she encountered; my mother remained relentlessly active in her mission to change lives for the better. Her life serves as a profound source of inspiration for me, as I had the privilege of witnessing her struggles up close. Yet, it's clear that she thrived on the challenges she encountered, using them as fuel for her unwavering commitment to making a difference.

Just before a devastating earthquake struck our region, we were facing a crisis. However, due to the goodwill and trust my mother had cultivated over the years and her readiness to take on any challenge, she had garnered the support of numerous backers who contributed to fundraising efforts for the relief activities she had meticulously planned. While my visits were limited to four villages, my mother journeyed to a staggering fifteen locations, providing aid and rebuilding a collapsed health center in Dhading.

Her ability to reach the most challenging and remote areas and support the neediest individuals exemplified her resilience. Yet again, in the face of adversity, she persevered and thrived, becoming a beacon of hope and empowerment for those she touched along her remarkable journey. Her unwavering commitment to creating positive change is a profound testament to the power of resilience.

Is it not our struggles that shape and define us? Our struggles transform us into better versions of ourselves. It is our natural tendency to resist change, to run from the battles and stay in our comfort zone, but the struggle transforms us. You need to have the belief and the courage to fight for what you believe in. Having the will and the courage to face struggles is another important aspect of creating resilience.

Developing Resilience

It's the sacrifices and struggles that help build resilience. And it's with resilience you rebuild yourself. It's not something you can train so easily, but it is something, like experience, that develops over time. It's like how a sword is forged. A sword becomes strong enough for its purpose only when it passes through a series of beating and exposure to high degrees of temperature. Similarly, the experience of the struggles and losses helps develop resilience. It's through the crucible of endurance that strength is forged.

In my journey, it became abundantly clear that resilience was not a passive trait but a dynamic force that could be cultivated through experience and action. Initially, when the first earthquake struck, fear and uncertainty consumed me. However, as I ventured on numerous trips and encountered events that demanded my advocacy and support for others, I found myself confronting my deepest fears with newfound determination. These experiences transformed me into a person who was less bound by fear and more driven by fearlessness.

Remarkably, this transformation wasn't unique to me; it extended to the communities and individuals I've visited. Over time, people within these communities became attuned to the needs and challenges of their fellow inhabitants. They embraced what they had lost and adapted to their new realities. This transformation was nothing short of remarkable; it was a process of developing a profound endurance, a resilience that was etched into their very being.

The rebuilding process transcended the physical reconstruction of infrastructures, buildings, and communities. It encompassed the intricate realms of psychology, emotion, and social dynamics. Resilience was being nurtured within individuals and communities alike. It was a combination of factors - the confrontation of fears, the unwavering support for others, the ability to adapt to change, and the multifaceted rebuilding process - crafting resilience in these regions' people.

As individuals grappled with their losses, adjusted to the new realities thrust upon them, and actively engaged in relief and reconstruction efforts, they simultaneously forged psychological and emotional resilience. This newfound strength allowed them to manage stress effectively, navigate challenging emotions, and maintain an unwavering positive outlook despite their adversities. The development of resilience wasn't just a byproduct of their experiences; it was a deliberate and powerful response to adversity, demonstrating the incredible capacity of individuals and communities to endure and thrive in the face of profound challenges.

In essence, my experiences and the efforts of the communities I worked with highlight how resilience was being built holistically. It involved addressing fears, empowering individuals and communities, adapting to change, developing endurance, fostering social connections, and rebuilding psychologically and emotionally. Through these processes, I and the communities I interacted with developed a deeper resilience that allowed me to navigate the complexities of post-earthquake challenges.

My decision to write about how Nepalese Society portrayed resilience during the earthquake is a way to document history and inspire and educate others. By sharing these stories, I can provide insights into the practical steps, mindset shifts, and communal efforts contributing to resilience-building. This can be a valuable resource for individuals, communities, and organizations seeking to enhance their capacity to navigate challenges, adapt to changes, and thrive in adversity. Resilience is not just a trait; it's a dynamic process that can be cultivated and nurtured through shared experiences, stories, and lessons like the ones I have just shared.

"Resilience is knowing that you are the only one that has the power and the responsibility to pick yourself up."

~ Mary Holloway

CHAPTER ELEVEN

Cultivating Resilience and Reclaiming Your Authentic Self

By Barbara Morris Jensen

Growing up in a highly dysfunctional family layered with trauma, chaos, and abuse, I separated from my true self at a very young age. Numbness, confusion, and emptiness became my way of being. However, little did I know there was still a resilient part of me that remained tucked away, waiting for the opportunity to emerge. Three pivotal moments changed the trajectory of my life.

The first moment was when my father casually asked me what I wanted to do when I grew up. I answered, "I want to be a psychologist," as I thought *Duh, doesn't everybody know what they want to do?* I later learned this wasn't all that common.

Just three years later, at the age of 16, my brother asked me where I wanted to attend college. I replied, "I'm too stupid to go to college." Strangely, even though I knew I wanted to be a psychologist, this was the furthest thing from my mind. After enduring abuse when I was younger, along with bullying at school, I lived in survival mode, detached from my emotions and blocked from my memories. My experiences were buried in a place into which I no longer had access. However, that all changed abruptly and painfully, and I was about to learn resilience the hard way.

By my mid-twenties I'd been married, had two children, worked at a bank, and was living a life created out of an unrealistic fantasy, without any sense of how to facilitate the steps and stages of life in a healthy, cohesive way. I would later discover this year would bring the beginning of a great awakening.

My father, the person I was closest to and loved dearly, died suddenly. I was crushed, desperate, and wanted to die. The realization dawned upon me that the aspect I had developed to shield myself from past wounds was destined to fade away, ultimately reawakening my authentic and resilient self.

All I had wanted of my father's belongings were his books. He was an intelligent man who had become a wise and awakened man after his own life-altering experience. While gathering his books, I found a psychology book, and my early memory of declaring I would be a psychologist came flooding back. I took this book to my brother and said, "I want to be a psychologist." His reply was, "How old will you be in five years? Will you be five years older with or without that degree?"

I was at a crossroads. Continue with an unhappy and unhealthy marriage, or trust life and follow what I'd known I was called to do all along. Once again, the change was drastic. No preparation. Trial by fire ensued. My marriage ended, and my two children and I were homeless. With no job and no family able to help me financially, I set out one blind step at a time, in the chaos of my mind and emotions, but also guided by something higher and greater that I hadn't even known I was in touch with.

I started college and found a part-time job. I was dedicated yet still sorting through the thoughts and emotions swirling around inside. Doubt and fear doubled down when my sister was killed in an accident leaving behind my 3-year-old niece, who shortly thereafter became my third child. I questioned how I could possibly work, care for my three children, and apply to graduate school while scraping the barrel financially, and regularly worrying about having enough food.

Amidst my desperation, my unyielding desire to persevere burned brightly within me, even as the shadows of uncertainty clouded the path ahead. The resilient part of me kept nudging me forward.

On the morning of my college interview, I dropped to my knees and said, "I need a sign." That's all I could utter. I pulled out a jewelry box from under my bed with my fake jewelry, resembling how fake I felt about my abilities to achieve what my heart had called me to. I opened the box, and what lay on top shocked me. It stopped me. It took my breath away.

On top of all the fake jewels was my father's medallion, with his spiritual master's picture, that he'd worn each day from the time he had awakened until the day he passed away. My sister had lost the medallion eight years prior, and it now appeared face up, on top of jewelry that I used most days. My sign. From that day forward, I trusted I was being guided, though from where I still did not know. But it didn't matter. It guided; I followed.

I have been a psychologist for more than 20 years and am deeply passionate and grateful to serve others and guide them back to their true selves, just as I was guided back to my own. In life, pivotal junctures emerge, demanding a choice: to tread the divergent road and distance oneself or to embark on the course aligning with their innate direction and inner resilience while navigating this journey.

As my father wisely said, "Every person, on the day they are born, has a gift-wrapped box laid at their feet, and very few will choose to open it." The question is… Will you?

“The key to life is resilience. We will always be knocked down. It’s the getting up that counts.”

~ Dominique Browning

CHAPTER TWELVE

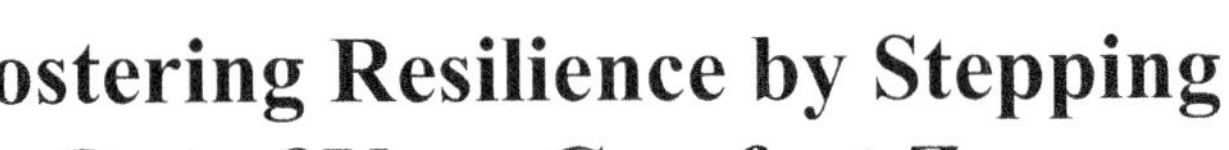

Fostering Resilience by Stepping Out of Your Comfort Zone

By John Spender

I found myself one early morning, aching with fatigue, my hand mechanically swirling a spoon in my Milo, tears silently tracing their paths down my cheeks. The grind of each dawn had become a relentless battle, one in which I'd lost track of the countless times I'd summoned sheer willpower to escape the cocoon of my bed. It was my way of leaving behind an old reality, driven by a burning desire to prove my worth.

Back then, a clear vision of my destination was an elusive wisp of possibility. Without it, I doubted I could muster the resilience necessary to persistently push myself beyond the cozy embrace of my comfort zone. There were mornings when all I yearned for was to surrender to the solace of my bed and shut out the world.

Yet, this fear of stagnation stoked the fires of motivation within me. I glimpsed the precipice of a life marred by endless nights of binge drinking and hazy encounters with pot—a directionless, uninspiring, and dangerous existence. Simultaneously, a magnetic force drew me towards the wonders of nature, the vastness of outdoor spaces, and the nurturing embrace of horticulture.

Life's challenges are unpredictable and often relentless storms that sweep through our lives. They test our resolve, question our abilities, and push us to the brink of surrender. In these moments of turmoil, the concept of resilience takes center stage, demonstrating its unparalleled significance in our lives. In this chapter, I invite you to embark on a deeply personal and introspective journey through the corridors of my own life, where resilience has emerged as a beacon of hope and strength.

Resilience is not an innate quality that some are blessed with and others lack; instead, it's a skill that can be cultivated and nurtured over time. It's the art of bouncing back from adversity, finding strength in the face of despair, and embracing the lessons that hardship offers. Like many others, my life has been marked by setbacks, obstacles, and moments of depression. However, it is precisely these experiences that have shaped my understanding of resilience and its transformative power.

In the following pages, I will share my struggles and triumphs, the pivotal moments that have tested my resolve. We will explore the psychological and emotional facets of resilience, the role of mindset and self-care, the importance of seeking support and connection, and the value of adaptability in the ever-changing landscape of our lives.

I encourage you to reflect on your experiences, challenges, and victories. Let my story be a source of inspiration and guidance as we embark on this quest to unlock the profound resilience within each of us. Together, we'll discover that no matter how dark the clouds may seem, there is always a way to find strength, hope, and a path forward.

Life's intricate dance often pivots on the focal point of timing. When my affluent Aunt Edwina called with a big opportunity, I found myself at the crossroads of longing for a transformative change, one overflowing with the promise of broadening my horizons far beyond my immediate view.

This encouraging opportunity was a program called "TAFE HSC Pathways." It entailed repeating year 11 and immersing myself once more in the conventional subjects of mathematics, English, and geography, all while embarking on a parallel journey into the world of horticulture.

My mother resided on the Central Coast, a two-hour journey encompassing buses and trains, five days a week, to reach the bustling heart of Sydney. The day I received the news of my acceptance into this two-year program remains etched in my memory, an exciting time for which I shall stay eternally thankful.

This marked the imminent transformation of the adversity of emotional, physical, and sexual abuse into resilience. This metamorphosis would equip me to navigate the arduous terrain of rigorous study and the daily commute between home and the corridors of learning.

Amidst the waves of change, my first year proved to be the backbone of my resilience. Armed with unwavering dedication and a never-say-die positive attitude, I forged ahead. The challenges were formidable, but my resolve remained unshaken.

In the realm of horticulture, I ascended to the pinnacle of each class. Even in the more conventional subjects like mathematics and English, I found myself in the top five. These accomplishments, however, were not just solitary feats of determination; they were the fruits of a collaborative effort—a testament to the strength of my support system.

The realization that resilience is not a solitary pursuit became evident. It wasn't just my strength that propelled me forward; it was the unwavering belief and encouragement of my teachers and family that sustained me through moments of doubt and fatigue.

Yet, a pivotal moment awaited on the horizon. With Oz-study payments, my dad's child support, and the toil of Wednesdays and Saturdays spent working for my uncle's friend's landscaping company, the dream of relocating to Sydney close to the TAFE college crystallized. This decision wasn't mine alone; it was a collective endeavor, a testament to the support that believed in me and provided the foundation upon which my resilience was built.

Seeking Guidance and Mentorship

I knew that to make this opportunity work, I had to use my resilience as a springboard to excel and endure the long study hours. The first year, I studied on the train rides to and from college. While the horticulture subjects were easier to become motivated about, applying myself to math, English, and geography was harder. I found that when you are resilient and persist through challenges, guidance and mentorship find you.

The intelligence that pervades all things is here to support us, even when things go against our limited expectations, and usually, the harder the challenge, the more resilience we'll need to push through to our full potential. It also means engaging in tasks we may not feel motivated for in order to achieve our objective.

During this time, I developed strong bonds with my math, English, and landscape construction teachers. My math teacher, Mr. Thaft, although he had bad breath, a short, plump stature, and was close to sixty, loved all things mathematics and cared about us learning to the best of our abilities. I often talked to him after class; he made me feel like an equal. He even hired me to redo some of his gardens and plant flowering plants for his wife. He often shared his problems with me and asked what I would do in certain situations he faced. I've always felt empowered in his presence.

My English teacher, Miss Williams, was well-traveled and had lived in the UK and Canada. She was also pushing sixty but was very young at heart and full of vibrant energy. She was ready to go the extra mile for the class while maintaining a lightness and grace in teaching. Miss Williams loved a bit of tongue-in-cheek banter and was quick to laugh. She often assisted at the after-hours study sessions and constantly instilled belief in me. I hadn't learned how to read and write at a basic level until I was nine, and I found it challenging to understand the grammatical rules. Her motto was that passing my exams was necessary but not taking them too seriously and forgetting to live life.

We called our practical landscape teacher by his first name, Ralph. He was super chilled and owned a landscape business, loved his family and surfing. He was patient, witty, good at breaking down tasks, and eager to teach, making sure that everyone knew how to complete the job at a satisfactory level of competence. He also didn't mind cheeky banter and a joke or two. We did a half day of practical training with him every week for two years, and during that first year, he would often drop me at Gosford train station, which was only 30 minutes from my mum's place. We would talk the whole way about general life topics and his family.

Throughout the duration of the program, I was fortunate to have these exceptional teachers by my side. While I held a genuine appreciation for my geography teacher and the other dedicated horticultural teachers, I forged profound connections with these particular educators over those two transformative years. Their unwavering belief in me and their trust in my abilities were the backbone of my resilience. Their steadfast support bolstered my enduring self-belief, giving me the strength and motivation to attend after-school study sessions consistently.

During my educational journey, these teachers became the weavers of my resilience, threading together a network of unwavering support and encouragement. Their mentorship went far beyond the classroom, extending into the realms of life itself. Through their guidance, I learned sturdiness isn't just about enduring challenges and fostering belief in one's potential. These educators were pivotal in nurturing my ability to bounce back from setbacks and persevere in adversity. This lesson would stay with me long after those formative years. My chapter is a testament to the profound impact their belief had on shaping my path toward resolve and self-assuredness.

When I successfully completed the TAFE HSC Pathway program, I had the skills and knowledge of a second-year apprentice, gaining employment first with the council for a year, then with a landscaping firm for six months, and with the support of my mom, I started my own business at 21. It was my resilience to show up early and be the last to leave in the early days of working with the council that led me to build unshakeable confidence, the ability to network with the right people giving me a helping hand along the way. This trend continues today as we connect with budding authors worldwide, publishing books like this, memoirs, and anthology books. Resilience is a muscle quickly weakened if we don't consistently challenge ourselves to do more and be more. Seeking guidance, mentorship, and networking is a valuable strategy for developing inner strength. If you wish to create anything worthwhile in life, you'll need the support of other people. If you remember the last time you struggled or worked towards a goal, did you do it alone? If you stop and think about it, I bet you had at least a little bit of support here and there, right? It often feels like we are living the journey of life solo, but if you stop and ponder, you realize that you had a helping hand here and there without you even asking.

I've learned that when we ask for support and guidance, people want to help; of course, we can develop resilience by trying to do everything ourselves, but often, this strategy isn't sustainable in the long term, leading to burnout and loneliness. It's not a weakness to ask for support—if anything, it takes more courage and resilience to allow others to support us. The next step is to work with a mentor, teacher, coach, and anyone with the knowledge you need to reach your desired outcome. Through mentorship, I've gained confidence, embraced challenges as opportunities, and developed the skills necessary to bounce back from setbacks. The mentor-mentee relationship fosters growth and a network of support, reminding us that we are not alone in our struggles. It is a dynamic partnership that fortifies our ability to adapt, learn, and thrive in the face of life's challenges, ultimately forging a resilient spirit that creates momentum from which we can live an abundant life.

Here are five strategies that enabled me to create resilience and to keep going when things were challenging:

- **Identify Role Models and Mentors:** Seek out individuals who have faced challenges similar to what you're experiencing or striving to overcome. These role models and mentors can offer valuable insights, advice, and support based on their experiences. Look for people who inspire you and are willing to share their knowledge and expertise.
- **Build a Diverse Network:** Don't limit yourself to just one mentor or source of guidance. Connect with a diverse network of people offering different perspectives and expertise. Surround yourself with knowledge and the people who foster and support your growth.
- **Ask for Feedback:** Actively seek feedback from mentors and teachers. Constructive feedback can help you identify areas for improvement and guide you in overcoming challenges. Be open to feedback and view it as an opportunity for growth. I've discovered that many people want us to win if we can receive their insights. Simply take what resonates and leave the rest.
- **Set Clear Goals and Expectations:** When seeking guidance and mentorship, be clear about your goals and expectations. Define what you hope to achieve and communicate this to your mentors. Clear goals can help you and your mentors focus on the most relevant areas for development.
- **Pay It Forward:** As you benefit from the guidance and mentorship of others, consider giving back by mentoring someone else. Sharing your experiences and knowledge not only helps others but can also reinforce your learning and resilience. It's a way to create a positive cycle of support and growth.

Keep in mind that seeking guidance and mentorship is a two-way process. It's necessary to be proactive, respectful, and appreciative of the time and expertise your mentors provide. Building strong relationships can significantly enhance your resilience by providing you with valuable guidance and a sense of support during challenging times.

My dad taught me resilience is enhanced when we forget our problems and help others. When he was diagnosed with Parkinson's disease, he was in denial. He was down in the dumps and retired from his job, which gave so much meaning to his life. One of the turning points was when he started mentoring kids who were struggling at school. It gave him a sense of purpose, and making a difference made my dad feel good about himself. It took resilience to subjugate his own challenges and be there for someone else.

The recent passing of my father due to his health challenges marked a profound and sad moment in my life. It was a poignant experience as I stood before the gathering at his funeral, paying tribute to his memory by reading the eulogy. The pain of his loss was palpable, yet within that sorrow, an unexpected glimmer of hope and fortitude emerged.

Among those deeply affected by my father's passing was a young teenager he had once mentored. Learning of my father's demise, this teenager experienced a complex mix of emotions, encompassing both sadness and gratitude. However, the transformative journey this young individual had undertaken was inspiring. Initially, he had been a troubled juvenile delinquent, seemingly headed down a challenging path in life. But my father's mentorship had sparked a remarkable change. Over time, the teenager shifted his focus, finding a newfound love for learning and nurturing a solid aspiration to become an engineer.

This transformation serves as a poignant testament to resilience, illustrating how, even in the face of loss, we can find the inner strength to overcome obstacles, redefine our focus, and embark on a path toward a brighter and more promising future. My father's legacy lives on not only in my heart but also in the lives he touched and inspired, reminding us all of the enduring power of resilience.

Another moment that touched my heart was at the wake when the pastor and I started chatting. As we shared memories of my dad, I'll never forget the last thing he said to me. He looked at me and said, "Will you take the baton?" At first, I was taken aback, unsure of what he meant. With a warm smile, he explained, "You know, in a relay race, athletes pass the baton. Your father has passed the baton to you, so what will you do with it?"

This unexpected metaphor has since become a powerful source of motivation in my life. Whenever I grapple with reluctance or hesitation, especially when faced with daunting tasks like writing this chapter, I am reminded of the symbolic baton my father had entrusted to me. It serves as a constant reminder of my responsibility and the knowledge that my actions can bring a smile to my dad's face in heaven. This fuels my determination and helps me push through challenges. The profound moment with the pastor has become a driving force, inspiring me to carry on and make the most of life's opportunities, just as my father would have wanted.

In my interconnected stories of resilience, I hope you see the profound truth: resilience not only helps us weather life's storms but also empowers us to make a positive difference in the lives of others. It's a reminder that even in the face of loss, we can find the inner strength to overcome, transform, and carry on, leaving a legacy that inspires others. As you move forward in your journey, may you carry the lessons of resilience: the acceptance of change, the embrace of responsibility, the pursuit of purpose, and the willingness to extend a helping hand.

I hope in return that you are open to the hands others extend to help you. Through these connections and relationships, we can forge a resilient spirit that encourages a sense of collaboration in the face of adversity. Lastly, let us be mindful of the unexpected sources of motivation that may come our way, like the symbolic baton my father passed to me.

"Finding gratitude and appreciation is key to resilience. People who take the time to list things they are grateful for are happier and healthier."

~ Sheryl Sandber

AUTHOR BIOGRAPHIES

AJ Myers

CHAPTER ONE

AJ, Founder of Heart2Pen, applies her Master Transformational Life Coach certification, education, and her life experiences to lift others up. Ms. Myers hands-on involvement with her community includes a position as Youth Prevention Coordinator to foster and teach healthy relationships of all types. She loves knowing that through her written words, utilizing Emotional Intelligence and NLP Skills, she can provide a platform for success.

For her accomplishments in the field, Ms. Myers has received numerous awards solidifying her business acumen bonded with compassionate kindness towards others. She has spent much of her time with organizations fighting world hunger and AIDs in Africa. Civically, she spent her time as a mentor for at-risk children.

Ms. Myers continues applying her heart-centered words to inspire people around the world to achieve their best. Balance between outdoor activities such as hiking, hunting, gardening, golfing, and scuba-diving vs her indoor passions of cooking/baking, painting in various mediums, and watching inspiring movies, keeps AJ centered.

Her authored works on rising after falling and leading by example: *A Journey of Riches-Abundant Living and Messages from the Heart* skyrocketed to #1 Best Selling books in the international market. *Creating Resilience* in this same world-renowned series is to be released, soon. Global publications feature AJ's inspiring works. She is currently working to complete and publish her manuscript for Book one of four of her novel series while she continues with the sequels. She is looking forward to *Life in Poetry* being released.

LinkedIn: www.linkedin.com/in/ajm6270

Email: 1heart2pen@gmail.com

Lars Johansen

CHAPTER TWO

Lars has a varied background from working and studying marketing and leadership to becoming an entrepreneur building a furniture brand – and now a licensed transformative coach, mentor and trainer. He brings the depth and range of his experience to his work and continues to be a lifelong student. Lars is passionate about helping and guiding people wake up to their true nature so they can live fully. With more peace of mind, inner freedom, and a deeper experience of unconditional love in their hearts.

In 2019, he stumbled across a completely new way of understanding how human beings create their experience of anxiety and how to dissolve it almost effortlessly. Apart from writing articles, blogs and books, Lars also runs the podcast 'What If Life Is Simpler Than We Think. ‹ More info can be found on his website www.larsjohansen.no.

Kirsten Heynisch

CHAPTER THREE

From an early age, Kirsten has been curious and passionate about understanding human nature, which is why she became a psychologist. She acquired a deep psychological understanding of human nature on her journey of learning, healing, and growing. Studying, practicing, while also being actively engaged in individual therapy, group therapy and coaching as a client for many years adds richness, liveliness, depth, and substance to her own life and her work as a psychologist and coach.

Kirsten's passion for psychology, coaching and learning has led her to complete two master's degrees (Leipzig University, Germany & City University, London) studying clinical, counselling & organizational psychology.

As a clinical psychologist, leadership & life coach, Kirsten enjoys the privilege and pleasure of sharing her learning with her clients, whom she supports and guides along their journey of navigating personal and professional challenges, struggles, trauma, and loss - creating resilience and profound transformation along the way.

Kirsten works with people from all walks of life, mainly with professionals, entrepreneurs, business owners and leaders. Her work is grounded in evidence-based methods from clinical psychology, organizational psychology, leadership psychology, neuroscience & coaching.

You can contact Kirsten directly:

Email: psychologypractice@kirstenheynisch.co.uk

Website: www.kirstenheynisch.co.uk

LinkedIn: www.linkedin.com/in/kirsten-heynisch-a25a19101/

Facebook: www.facebook.com/profile.php?id=100010237200988

You can access Kirsten's Free Welcome Pack here: https://mailchi.mp/49e05e0f052d/aqvwag769a

It contains Two Videos & an Audio, which will introduce you to some vital steppingstones in the process of cultivating Inner Balance, Peace of Mind & Resilience.

Diana Elena Matei

CHAPTER FOUR

Diana Elena Matei is a woman of many hats that loves being in the NOW.

She is a daughter of God, D. Intuitive Coach, a holistic and transformational practitioner, Reiki Master, Oracle Reader, Crystal & Chakra Healer, Angelic Therapist, Certified Moonologist, Magic Numerolgist, the host of Shine Your Light Unapologetically Podcast (now in Top 10% global!) and so much more.

D. Intuitive Coach is an aspect of herself as Diana holds the space for women ready to grieve the losses they have experienced in the past and transform them into future wins by creating resilience and practicing forgiveness while having a gratitude attitude. After hiding in the spiritual closet for almost two decades while avoiding pain of any kind, Diana is now embodying the Light that she is. She is shining her Light unapologetically knowing that the right vibrational match for her energy is going to reach out whenever ready to embark on a journey of riches. Witnessing her clients 'transformation' is Diana's cosmic reward.

Will it be easy? No. Because growth does not start at the core of your comfort zone. But it starts with your decision. Right here. Right now.

Corrina Andersen

CHAPTER FIVE

Sydney-based interior designer and entrepreneur Corrina Carmen Andersen has been designing high-end residences and commercial spaces for the past twenty years.

Corrina's interior design has been featured in many major lifestyle publications and TV networks including Foxtel Lifestyle Channel, Home Beautiful Magazine, Modern Home, Australian Home Ideas, Kitchen and Bathrooms and Sydney Morning Herald 'Home' to name but a few.

With a personal interest in holistic health and well-being, Corrina recently turned her attention to holistic design, wanting to make a difference in her client's environment, creating calming, relaxing and sacred spaces. With a personal philosophy that if a person is out of balance, their life is out of balance as well. She uses her intuitive skills to help others.

Corrina has travelled extensively, experiencing her passion for Japanese architecture and the calmness of Zen gardens, first-hand as well as the deserts of Palm Springs with a particular fondness for mid-century designs.

A devotee to her daily meditation practices and daily ocean walks Corrina draws on her own experience to write poetry in her spare time and has designed her lifestyle brand and plans on extending her range shortly.

Corrina has a diploma in Advanced Counselling, Holistic Design and Feng Shui.

Ominda Soemidjadi

CHAPTER SIX

Ominda was born in Australia to an Australian mother and an Indonesian father. She now resides in a small village in the UK near the beautiful British seaside.

Ominda has been working in the Mental Health sector for over eight years and has a personal professional passion and interest in Mental Health. She has suffered and learnt to live with PTSD herself.

This is Ominda's first published writing project. She hopes her life experiences and future work will be a way to deliver her message and help someone in their life or inspire others.

Ominda hopes her experiences in creating resilience will help others on their own journeys and has found this journey a therapeutic experience.

This is her first piece of writing after many years of composing stories, and if you are interested in more of Ominda's future work or would like to connect with her please email omindap@hotmail.co.uk

Jon Ch. Henningsen

CHAPTER SEVEN

Jon Ch. Henningsen is a health coach/lifestyle mentor with an educational background in sports nutrition and performance optimization.

He owns a small gym in Denmark, where he shares his passion for resistance training, nutrition, self-development, and preventative lifestyle medicine principles.

Jon blends scientific insight with practical advice to help people (strong/functional with maximum quality of life and maximum health-span).

He specializes in mentoring cancer patients, habit change, fat loss, and why nutrition quality and muscle mass/strength are important.

His transformational journey, losing over 20 kg with lifestyle changes after a cancer diagnosis in 2013 (keeping off the fat for over a decade by now/overcoming backpain, allergies and pre-diabetes in the process), powerfully spills over as a foundational element in his coaching method.

Jon's own transformative experience fuels his dedication to help others by advocating personal responsibility (value of active role-models) and living healthy as a means of disease prevention.

He broke a world record in 2020 without knowing it (https://www.recordholdersrepublic.co.uk/world-record-holders/1501/jon-ch_-henningsen.aspx).

Jon was the first to complete Denmark's longest official bike ride (375 km) on a mountain bike (2012).

Lead By Example (leadbyexample.online) is his online coaching business for English-speakers.

Jon is a family-man, an admirer of nature, supporter of regenerative agriculture, a heavy metal enthusiast, a coin collector, a writer of poetry, and has followed SSC Napoli since 1986.

His teachings serve as a testament to the power of resilience, gratitude and dedication, encouraging people that step into his eco-system to take control of their health, one step at a time.

Inez Cooke

CHAPTER EIGHT

Inez captures the sublime and makes the ordinary extraordinary!

She started her adventurous career in the arts nearly 30 years ago, having completed her studies in Art and Design at the University of Hertfordshire in the UK. Gaining a variety of skills in multiple creative fields so as to not get pigeon-holed, Inez went on to design textile prints for the international fashion design market, selling designs to Ralph Lauren and Etam Paris.

Taking a career break for a year to travel around Australia, Inez returned to the UK and moved to Bristol a flourishing city and where the internationally renowned street artist Banksy is from.

After her own successful show exhibiting scenes of Bristol, people started to ask for commissioned pieces. Painting portraits of their homes Inez captures the sublime and makes the ordinary extraordinary.

Inez works in a range of styles and mediums always wanting to give herself new challenges so to keep her passion flowing and her work fresh and lively. She works intuitively enjoying a hyperreal pallet likes the colors on a hot summer's day. Her main medium is gouache paint it gives a vibrancy and vitality that has a velvety chalkiness feel.

Her latest commission was for a print design for merchandise, for The Mansion House Museum in York.

You can find her at www.inezcooke.com, Instagram: @inezmarycrayon, Facebook: Inez Cooke

Emily Kane

CHAPTER NINE

Emily Kane is a Naval Officer (Ret.) residing in Colorado Springs, CO. She has a BS and MS in Computer Sciences and Communications. While growing up in a small farming community in Iowa, she developed a passion for traveling, writing, and learning about natural and self-healing modalities.

Through her extensive travels, she was introduced to wonderful people, places, and situations all over the world. These opportunities have also enabled her to appreciate working with diverse people of numerous cultures. Additionally, she possesses an abiding love and appreciation for nature and animals.

While serving in the Navy and living abroad, she raised her family and continued writing on subjects of interest to the community and at the various bases she served. Emily also possesses an entrepreneurial spirit as the founder of Emily's Elegant Essentials where she empowers others with her talents to showcase several ways to wear jewelry with their daily attire to highlight their internal beauty and self-confidence.

Sagar Bahadur Dhakal

CHAPTER TEN

Sagar Bahadur Dhakal is a software engineer based in Pokhara, Nepal with an MBA in Global Leadership and Management. Right after his high school, together with his mother Mrs. Goma Dhakal, he has played an instrumental role in setting up and managing an orphanage which has supported more than 200 children at different points in their life securing residential, academic, education, health, and other basic securities of life since 2007. Similarly, they also operate a rewarding social enterprise for women, a handicraft manufacturing small scale industry where they provide training and income opportunities for disadvantaged women since 2010.

After receiving his engineering diploma from Tribhuvan University, Sagar, also working part time as a freelance web developer, again joined his family to set up a farm and a homestay in Pokhara, with the objective of producing organic food as well as trying to create a link between agriculture and tourism, since both sectors touch the lives of majority of people in Nepal.

After three years of developing the project, he pursued an MBA degree in Global Leadership and Management, a joint degree program from Tribhivan University and Handong Global University, with the latter organizing intensive camps for development of social enterprises.

Currently, playing a crucial role in all these projects, he also works as a freelance webapp developer as well as digital marketing and SEO agency for small local businesses together with some of the grown up children from the orphanage who have been training under him for a few years.

Barbara Morris Jensen

CHAPTER ELEVEN

Barbara Morris Jensen, Doctor of Clinical Psychology, Clinical Hypnotherapist and Certified Life Coach, has dedicated her career to helping people live meaningful and fulfilling lives. Her compassion and ability to quickly tune into the deeper dynamics that underlie the challenges people face, makes her a reliable resource for lasting change and helping people find their true path.

She uses hypnotherapy and solution-focused skills to help her patients and clients recognize and upgrade their subconscious beliefs that have held them back and kept them stuck, and to free them from the pain of the past.

Her interest developed from a deep desire to free herself from depression, anxiety and lack of self-worth. Determined to eliminate negative and restrictive core beliefs and emotional pain, she has sought to understand subconscious beliefs and patterns that affect personal and professional relationships. As a result, she rewired her mental blueprint and emotional patterns, and has designed a genuine life aligned with her desires. She now uses this process to intimately and effectively help individuals, couples, and businesses connect to their own intrinsic value.

Her approach assists in creating meaningful and lasting change through re-processing and re-evaluating outdated mental patterns and emotional cycles and restoring connection with the authentic self. She's been called the Soul Whisperer with her ability to notice and draw out the true nature of others and help them develop and live an authentic life.

Her passion is to inspire, guide and uplift those willing to walk the awakening path, to break the barriers and evolve beyond self-imposed limits. This change, this restructuring of the mind to connect with the soul, is what she calls the Soul Revolution.

John Spender

CHAPTER TWELVE

John Spender is a 34-time International Best-Selling co-author, who didn't learn how to read and write at a basic level until he was ten years old. He has since traveled to more than 70 countries, territories and started many businesses leading him to create the best-selling book series *A Journey Of Riches*. He is an Award-Winning International Speaker and Movie Maker.

John worked as an international NLP trainer and coached thousands of people from various backgrounds through many challenges. From the borderline homeless to wealthy individuals, he has helped many people to connect with their truth to create a life on their terms.

John's search for answers to living a fulfilling life has taken him to work with Native American Indians in the Hills of San Diego, to visit the forests of Madagascar, swim with humpback whales in Tonga, explore the Okavango Delta of Botswana and climb the Great Wall of China. He's traveled from Chile to Slovakia, Hungary to the Solomon Islands, the mountains of Italy and the streets of Mexico.

Everywhere his journey has taken him, John has discovered a hunger among people to find a new way to live, with a yearning for freedom of expression. His belief that everyone has a book in them was born.

He is now a writing coach, having worked with over 300 authors from 40 countries for the *A Journey of Riches* series http://ajourneyofriches.com/ and his publishing house, Motion Media International, has published 44 non-fiction titles to date.

John also co-wrote and produced the movie documentary *Adversity* starring Jack Canfield, Rev. Micheal Bernard Beckwith, Dr. John Demartini and many more, coming soon in 2022. And you can bet there will be a best-selling book to follow!

“Resilience is not what happens to you. It’s how you react to, respond to, and recover from what happens to you.”

~ Jeffery Gitomer

AFTERWORD

I hope you enjoyed the shared heartfelt stories, wisdom, and vulnerability. Storytelling is the oldest form of communication, and I hope you feel inspired to take a step toward living a fulfilling life. Feel free to contact any of the authors in this book or the other books in this series.

The proceeds of this book will be used for social giving at Jewel Children's Home in Northeast Bali.

Other books in the series are...

Discover Your Purpose: A Journey of Riches, Book Thirty-three
https://www.amazon.com/dp/B0CFDLWTCB

Live Your Passion: A Journey of Riches, Book Thirty-two
https://www.amazon.com/Live-Your-Passion-Stories-Fulfilling-ebook/dp/B0C5QXMNRQ

Master Your Mindset: A Jour*ney of Riches*, Book Thirty-one
https://mybook.to/MasterYourMindset

Transform Your Wounds into Wisdom: A Journey of Riches, Book Thirty
https://www.amazon.com/dp/ B0BKTJ377N

Motivate Your Life: A Journey of Riches, Book Twenty-Nine
https://www.amazon.com/dp/B0BCXMF11P

Awaken to Your Inner Truth: A Journey of Riches, Book Twenty-Eight
https://www.amazon.com/dp/B09YLYMQ4H?geniuslink=true

Awaken to Your Inner Truth: A Journey of Riches, Book Twenty-Eight
https://www.amazon.com/dp/B09YLYMQ4H?geniuslink=true

The Power of Inspiration: A Journey of Riches, Book Twenty-Seven
http://mybook.to/ThePowerofInspiration

Messages from The Heart: A Journey of Riches, Book Twenty-Six
http://mybook.to/MessagesOfHeart

Abundant Living: A Journey of Riches, Book Twenty-Five
https://www.amazon.com/dp/B0963N6B2C

The Way of the Leader: A Journey of Riches, Book Twenty-Four
https://www.amazon.com/dp/1925919285

The Attitude of Gratitude: *A Journey of Riches,* Book Twenty-Three
https://www.amazon.com/dp/1925919269

Facing Your Fears: *A Journey of Riches,* Book Twenty-Two
https://www.amazon.com/dp/1925919218

Returning to Love: *A Journey of Riches,* Book Twenty-One
https://www.amazon.com/dp/B08C54M2RB

Develop Inner Strength: *A Journey of Riches,* Book Twenty
https://www.amazon.com/dp/1925919153

Building your Dreams: A Journey of Riches, Book Nineteen
https://www.amazon.com/dp/B081KZCN5R

Liberate your Struggles: A Journey of Riches, Book Eighteen
https://www.amazon.com/dp/1925919099

In Search of Happiness: A Journey of Riches, Book Seventeen
https://www.amazon.com/dp/B07R8HMP3K

Tapping into Courage: A Journey of Riches, Book Sixteen
https://www.amazon.com/dp/B07NDCY1KY

The Power Healing: A Journey of Riches, Book Fifteen
https://www.amazon.com/dp/B07LGRJQ2S

The Way of the Entrepreneur: A Journey Of Riches, Book Fourteen
https://www.amazon.com/dp/B07KNHYR8V

Discovering Love and Gratitude: A Journey Of Riches, Book Thirteen
https://www.amazon.com/dp/B07H23Q6D1

Transformational Change: A Journey Of Riches, Book Twelve
https://www.amazon.com/dp/B07FYHMQRS

Finding Inspiration: A Journey Of Riches, Book Eleven
https://www.amazon.com/dp/B07F1LS1ZW

Building your Life from Rock Bottom: A Journey Of Riches, Book Ten
https://www.amazon.com/dp/B07CZK155Z

Transformation Calling: A Journey Of Riches, Book Nine
https://www.amazon.com/dp/B07BWQY9FB

Letting Go and Embracing the New: A Journey Of Riches, Book Eight
https://www.amazon.com/dp/B079ZKT2C2

Making Empowering Choices: A Journey Of Riches, Book Seven
https://www.amazon.com/Making-Empowering-Choices-Journey-Riches-ebook/dp/B078JXMK5V

The Benefit of Challenge: A Journey Of Riches, Book Six
https://www.amazon.com/dp/B0778S2VBD

Personal Changes: A Journey Of Riches, Book Five
https://www.amazon.com/dp/B075WCQM4N

Dealing with Changes in Life: A Journey Of Riches, Book Four
https://www.amazon.com/dp/B0716RDKK7

Making Changes: A Journey Of Riches, Book Three
https://www.amazon.com/dp/B01MYWNI5A

The Gift In Challenge: A Journey Of Riches, Book Two
https://www.amazon.com/dp/B01GBEML4G

From Darkness into the Light: A Journey Of Riches, Book One
https://www.amazon.com/dp/B018QMPHJW

Thank you to all the authors who have shared aspects of their lives, hoping to inspire others to live a bigger version of themselves.

I want to share a beautiful quote from Jim Rohan, "You can't complain and feel grateful at the same time." At any given moment, we can either feel like a victim of life or be connected and grateful for it. I hope this book helps you feel grateful and inspires you to pursue your dreams.

For more information about contributing to the series, visit http://ajourneyofriches.com/. Furthermore, if you enjoyed reading this book, we would appreciate your review on Amazon to help get our message out to even more readers.

Printed in Great Britain
by Amazon

45484312R00129